CW00794546

Also Published by Ballantine Books:

BARRY MANILOW
BILLY IDOL
BILLY JOEL
BRUCE SPRINGSTEEN
CULTURE CLUB
CYNDI LAUPER
DURAN DURAN
EURYTHMICS
HALL AND OATES
HUEY LEWIS AND THE NEWS
JOHN COUGAR MELLENCAMP
JULIAN LENNON
THE PRETENDERS
PRINCE
STEVIE NICKS
STEVIE WONDER
STING AND THE POLICE
TINA TURNER
U2
VAN HALEN
ZZ TOP

WHAM!

by Darlene Fredricks

A **2M** Communications Production

BALLANTINE BOOKS • NEW YORK

Library of Congress Catalog Card Number: 85-90854

ISBN 0-345-32998-8

Manufactured in the United States of America

First Edition: January 1986

Front Cover photo: Chris Craymer/RDR Productions/Scope Features
Back Cover photo: Star File
Photo Research: Amanda Rubin
Interior Design: Michaelis/Carpelis Design Associates, Inc.

Dedicated to: Jack Lamb, a really nice guy to be
related to!
and
Diane, my best friend.

CONTENTS

ACKNOWLEDGMENTS

Thank you: Jim King, Suzan Colon, David, Drew Wheeler, the G., Doc Tom, Mom and Dad, and 2M Communications.

INTRODUCTION

*F*rom a "Careless Whisper" to a scream, Wham! have made it big and made things happen. Wham! are where it's at today: they're talented, they're sexy, they're magic, they're show business. Wham! thrill and chill, bringing a smile to your lips and a tear to your eye. You wouldn't swap them for anything else.

Wham! have come a long way. They weren't born rich and famous, but if you take one look at them you'll see that they were born to be rich and famous. They're cool and confident, and their stylish flair is as entertaining as their music. Something about George and Andrew demands that they reside in the perfect setting. Those stunningly handsome mugs and their classic friendship are like Hollywood come to life.

What is behind their storybook ascent to famedom? Where have these lovely boys been, and where are they going? Turn the page and see for yourself....

YORGI, PORGI, PUDDIN' AND PIE...

Yorgus Panaviotou, also known as George Michael Panos, was born on June 25, 1963, in Finchley, North London. His parents, Jack and Lesley, brought him into the world with a tight-knit and loving family behind him. George is the only boy in the family—he has two sisters named Yioda and Melanie. There was always plenty of affection in their home, and it taught George the sensitivity that is so evident in his songwriting today.

Jack is a very hardworking man with a strong sense of values. This Greek Cypriot immigrant worked his way up from waiter to restaurant owner, and he's justifiably proud of it. "My dad always believed that you had to work really

hard to get anywhere," George explained in *Bop*. Mom
Lesley pitched in by working as a secretary for a while
when George was in grammar school.

It's hard to believe that ultra-clean and well-ironed
George used to come home covered in dirt and grass
stains. It wasn't a case of a rambunctious Dennis the
Menace on the loose; curious George was merely fasci-
nated with nature. This interest led him over hill and dale
. . . but mostly it led him to a fence near his school. The
fence was his amateur laboratory. He wallowed in the
dirt, poking and prying in his search for exotic creatures,
like ants!

Actually, Lesley first discovered her son's budding talent because of this rather off-putting hobby. The young
collector would silently sneak from the house at six o'-
clock A.M. for an early-morning bug hunt. His searching
was done in a field across the street, so he didn't even
bother to change his clothes. One day a neighbor told
Lesley that her son did more in the field than chase crawling things; he sang while he worked! The neighbor commented on George's wonderful voice and his dress sense.
These concerts were performed in pajamas!

Perhaps George is such a dedicated worker today because of his disciplined upbringing. Sometimes Lesley
tells George that she might have been a bit *too* strict, but
he doesn't remember her that way. A spanking was her
way of showing that things had really gotten out of hand,
like the time the family was visiting Cyprus when George
was a boy.

Jack's family lived on the sunny island, and it was quite
a change from the damp and gloomy weather of Great

Britain. George has always loved sunshine, but no amount of it could offset a rather nasty occurrence, for George was caught stealing! He and a cousin had gone out for the day and managed to acquire a whole bunch of food by just helping themselves. They hid the food and thought everything was fine, until a guy came banging on the door! He made the boys show Lesley the booty, and she gave George a lesson applied directly to the back of his legs.

The spank marks and pain stayed around long enough to teach George that stealing wasn't worth all the hurt it caused. Now he's glad his mom cared enough to keep him from making other mistakes.

In fact, this hunky heartthrob is best friends with his mother for life. Their touching relationship has helped him over the rough spots of everyday existence, as well as the tremendous strain that comes with living in the public eye.

George always credits his mother with beauty. Not just physical beauty, but the kind of beauty flowing from inside. She loves her son and his music, and she always has a few words of encouragement for him when he's working. When things are going well for George, she gets nearly as enthusiastic as he does. "That means such a lot to me," stated George in *The News of the World Sunday Magazine*. "She can tell at once what will be a hit ... and what won't." Now we know who influences Wham!'s choice of singles!

When he's away on tour, George doesn't write often. It's not because he doesn't like to write.... It's because Lesley is usually on the road with him. The whole Michael family has been toted along to the most exotic locations with the boys. Before these generosities were possible, George explained, "I don't really need to write to her because we've got a direct line that goes heart-to-heart" *(The News of the World Sunday Magazine)*.

Even though Lesley worked occasionally when George was younger, she usually made it home to greet George when his classes were over. Her sporadic spankings were far outweighed by her hugs and kisses. She still cuddles George when he's down in the dumps, and these days he finds it easy to hug her back.

When he was younger it wasn't as simple. The whole Michael clan is extremely demonstrative, especially Mom. Younger kids often get embarrassed by hugging and kissing . . . especially boys! George was no exception, but he's grown out of dodging such attentions.

Lesley didn't exactly share George's enthusiasm for the musician's life. It seemed unstable and risky to say the least. She wanted her children to succeed, and her idea of success was an iron-clad career with a secure future. As George got more determined, she began to understand his degree of commitment. Years slipped by and his ambition hadn't wavered. Lesley decided to support him even though Jack still didn't like the idea.

Now that Wham! are the biggest sensation on four legs, Lesley is proud and pleased. It wasn't always this smooth. Back when George and Andrew formed their first band, she was more than a bit miffed. The boys constantly wanted to rehearse at the Michael house. Eventually she would let them, but not without trying to dissuade him.

Primarily, Lesley objected to the time George's musical activities took away from his school work. Once she was summoned to his school because of his grades, and she returned home crying. Afterward, she watched him to make sure he balanced his work and his "play."

Now she knows that it was not really play, and her only fear when Wham! started to get ahead was for George's ego. When she realized fame would not adversely affect her son—when George remained the sweet boy she'd raised—she stopped worrying.

George grew up in a well-run household and learned a lot about responsibility along the way. Instead of giving him a regular allowance, Lesley made him earn it by doing odd jobs for her. Now he understands the "whys and wherefores" of personal financial management, even if the money he earns now is quite a lot more than what he used to get for mowing the lawn. Mom also taught him to clean after himself, though he has claimed she pampers him these days.

This is a very special relationship, and as time goes on it gets stronger and stronger. Any candidate for George's affections had better take heed; Lesley will always have a place in her son's heart, a very important place that no one else can touch.

George's urge to sing and be involved in music came when he was very young. His parents had other ideas; they wanted him to be a lawyer. Nonetheless, they relented a little and gave him a tape recorder when he was seven. George taped Elton John records from the radio so he could listen to them over and over. Eventually he discovered an abandoned record player in the family garage. Stored with it was a pile of Motown albums. George spent a lot of time in the garage, listening to the sweet soul and heavy beat of the Motown sound, bands like the Temptations and the Supremes.

It's strange to think that these humble beginnings belong to one of the eighties' biggest superstars. George himself probably finds it odd from time to time. When he sang along with all those Motown records back in the early seventies, he had no notion that he would sing with Motown's biggest artists on the Apollo Theater stage someday.

When he was twelve, two new things came into his life. One was a drum kit to bash around with at home. It's a good thing George decided not to pursue drumming. Those huge drum sets hide the people behind them, and none of us want to see less of George's fabulous physique! Drummers don't get any chance to dance, either—another definite disadvantage.

George's drum kit led to trouble, because he played it instead of doing his schoolwork. He eventually tired of the drums, but the next change in his life stayed with him for good.

The family decided to move to the suburb of Bushey, Hertfordshire. It was in Bushey Meads High School that George met his best friend to be, Andrew Ridgeley.

ANDREW'S FIRST YEARS: A DIFFERENT KIND OF ROCK 'N' ROLL

Andrew John Ridgeley doesn't exactly play rock and roll, but these words accurately describe his on-the-go lifestyle. If you think he's a born rebel, you're absolutely right. Andrew is no newcomer to the "Young Guns" method of charging ahead regardless.

It all began on January 26, 1963, in the Windlesham Maternity Home. As time went on, Jenny and Albert Mario Ridgeley discovered their son's ability to get into trouble. His philosophy could be summed up with a twist of an old cliché: leap now, look later.

Jenny can trace this devil-may-care approach back to when Andrew was only two, when her nonstop son ran

straight into a pool! She was terrified for a few eternal
seconds, as only a mother can be, and rushed toward him.
Before she got to the edge, Andrew bobbed to the surface,
giggling his head off. You could say that Andrew's never
stopped jumping in at the deep end since, and Mrs. Ridgeley has claimed his love of water sports began with that
very first splash.

Plainly, Andrew doesn't believe in tentatively sticking
his toe into the waters of any situation. His parents tried
their best not to dampen his adventurous spirit, and he's
grateful. Like the Michael family, the Ridgeley crew are
still close.

Andrew's family has something else in common with
George's family: an exotic background. His father, Albert
Mario, is from Egypt, and Andrew's paternal grandfather
is an Arabian who took an Italian wife. Now you know
where Adorable Andy got his special brand of good looks!

And you can bet that all this adventure still left time
for more amorous thoughts. Andrew's first crush predated
his teen years. When he was five or six, he developed
some rather precocious yearnings for one of his mother's
friends, and he still gets a little flustered when he talks
about it.

A first crush isn't the same as first true love, and a
boy's first love is often not a person at all, much to the
distress of countless exasperated girls. Andrew's first love
was sports, especially football.

English football is the game we call soccer. You've
probably heard other British stars, like Def Leppard or
Duran Duran, mention the influence football had on their
youth. Most of them, including Andrew, still follow the

teams they support. If this doesn't seem very consistent with your picture of the pop life, then perhaps you're thinking in American.

Football players have been role models for energetic British boys since the sport became popular, decades ago. Long before pop music turned into the ticket to fame that it is today, young men saw football as a way to beat the British class system. Traditionally, British society is somewhat segregated by birth, rather than money. You can't really work your way into the upper class and the respect that comes from being born into the right family. There is a place for everyone, and everyone is faced with fitting into his place.

Naturally there are exceptions. Football provides an escape for working-class and middle-class boys who don't want to try their luck working their way through the system. Since the sport is based on reflexes and skill rather than brawn, so it's much easier to develop into a successful footballer in Britain. Men who play American football do work hard at their craft, but most are still endowed with a special something from birth: namely, the ability to produce an extra 175 pounds of rock-hard body weight!

English football players like Kenny Daglish and George Best illustrate the two kinds of football player a talented boy can become. They're both comfortable financially. They both sponsor products, go on television, and get into the papers. Kenny, who still plays for the Liverpool team, is more of the quiet type. Recently he received an OBE (Order of the British Empire), an award not often bestowed on sportsmen.

The British adore both kinds of footballer, and the wild

guys of the game certainly look glamorous with their nightclubbing, sports cars, champagne, and gorgeous girl-friends. The true stars are cheered on by the guys and sighed over by the girls (some of them rival pop music's prettiest hunks!). It's obvious that the soccer lifestyle has lots in common with the life that Andrew leads now, and it's easy to see why he was so drawn to football as a kid.

Active Andrew rung up more than the usual amount of childhood injuries. He's managed to break his nose twice! Add to that a broken arm, a fractured foot, and a dislocated knee and you've got the makings of an Andrew who rattles when he walks. Fortunately, he's kept himself together, and his war wounds haven't hindered his exciting onstage antics.

When the skateboarding craze made the scene in England, Andrew was presented with a whole new way to do himself grievous bodily harm. Although she believed in giving the bouncing boy room to run, Mom Jenny refused point blank when Andy asked for a skateboard of his own. The fact that the board in question cost a whopping sixty pounds didn't help much. So Andy chalked it all up to experience and went to work. He got himself a paper route and paid for the whole thing himself.

George and Andrew certainly are different, and their differences become super-apparent when you compare their childhoods. Why was George such an introvert and Andrew such an extrovert?

One reason for Andy's extrovert behavior could be his brother Paul. The two have always been totally competitive, jostling to beat each other out in sports and with the girls. They even try to compete with each other in the good looks department! So, while George grew up with two sweet sisters, Melanie and Yioda, Andrew was pitted against his younger brother Paul. Since Paul was born only thirteen months after Andrew, the competition is even keener.

The competition between the gorgeous Ridgeley brothers continues even today. Mr. Paul Ridgeley is a delicious dark-haired hunk in the first degree, classically handsome. Some Wham!sters will argue that Andrew's good looks are a shade more interesting; but whatever your opinion, you'll certainly welcome the chance to get to know a little about the second Ridgeley boy.

When one considers the brotherly rivalry of these two guys, it's not surprising that Paul doesn't go out of his way to lavish praise on his superstar sibling. In fact, he isn't on their long list of fans at all! Paul has stated that he wouldn't buy their records, because the Wham! sound is not exactly his cup of tea. It's not that he isn't into music; Paul is a drummer who has been working on his own projects for years, including a band called Physique. It's simply that Paul is not interested in a quick ride to fame on his brother's tartan coat tails. He's going to make it his own way, and his different musical tastes can only help him.

Wham!sters might find Paul's comments on Wham! a bit startling, but we must remember that it's all in the family. If Andrew doesn't mind what his brother says about his group, why should we? Paul is the first to admit that he really admires his big brother. It's hard to imagine that Andrew rescued Paul from a bully many years ago when you compare their sizes today. (Paul is a towering six feet, three inches!) Deeds like this are never forgotten, and they breed deep respect.

Paul never means to be unkind, only truthful. He assures everyone that he isn't jealous of his brother's success, because he's going to have a piece of success for himself one day. "I've got the talent, drive and ambition, but so far Andy's had the good breaks. Soon they'll start coming my way," confided Paul in *The News of the World*.

Paul even goes as far as proclaiming that he's a better musician than Andrew! "Being really honest, I think I'm more talented than Andy as a musician and a songwriter. . . . I'm better than him, but I still have to prove it," he told *The News of the World* in the same interview. Before you get your backs up about this, faithful Wham! fans, consider Andrew's position in the group. Actually, he has never made a big thing out of his playing ability or songwriting. Everybody knows that Andrew's talents lie in other directions, like his crowd-pleasing onstage presence. And *everybody* includes Andrew himself, and Paul, who goes on to affirm that Wham! wouldn't be Wham! without his brother.

Paul really sticks up for Andrew when people accuse him of not doing his fair share of work, and Andrew is pleased to receive such a vote of confidence. But while the two still get along okay, George and Paul have had a run-in or two. Without the temperance of brotherly affection, Paul's outspoken opinions of George can get downright critical! The Wham! men are smart enough not to let such things interfere with their relationship, so it doesn't do any harm.

Andrew and Paul still indulge in a little locker room

talk now and then. They enjoy talking about girls together. . . . After all, they've been doing it for years. Usually, they just swap stories and discuss different ways to flirt, because neither one of these playboy types has ever needed much "Dear Abby"–style advice when it comes to love.

When the Ridgeley boys used to come to blows, Paul's superior size assured him of an easy win. Andrew compensated by learning the power of clever arguing. Most heated discussions ended with Andrew the winner.

No matter how much these two volatile guys run head on into each other, they're still friends. Their rivalry also stays friendly, and Andrew is always willing to help Paul out with advice on music and the business world in general. The older Ridgeley is still pretty protective of his large little brother.

There's no contest when it comes to family feelings. In the Ridgeley house there's always plenty of love, enough for second helpings. Jenny puts some of her love into her cooking, and Andrew gives her heaps of praise for her roasts. Though he's not a dessert eater these days, Andy must have either done or *not* done something to his teeth when he was a boy. One of his trips to the dentist yielded a bumper crop of twelve fillings! He watches his mouth nowadays.

Did you know that advanced and naughty Andrew even started sleeping in the buff as a child? ". . . Because pajama bottoms ride up around your knees and the tops ride up around your stomach. I used to wake up with them all twisted and go AARGG." It's a good thing Andrew wasn't into the same morning activities as George. The neighbors would have been commenting on more than his singing!

Before George arrived, Andrew managed to get into plenty of trouble with other friends. On a school trip to Wales, the eleven-year-old imp got into a massive talcum powder fight with his classmates! Andrew was frantically cleaning up and hunting for a lost watch when he got a big surprise; a teacher walked in and whacked him one. Corporal punishment is still widely used in Britain, and while Andy was never bad enough to get caned, he got more than the usual amount of sessions with the slipper. The old soft shoe isn't so soft when it's applied to your backside!

As Andrew got older, he kept up his fast pace. This marathon sprint brought him colliding into his future partner in music, a very quiet boy named George Michael.

TOGETHER
FOREVER

*E*very day we see events that appear deceptively insignificant. Some people call it fate ... and others say much ruder things about it! In any case, it can be for the best, as well as for the worst.

Keep that in mind as you examine the silly and very chancy events that brought George Michael and Andrew Ridgeley together. Were it not for a bit of this and a sprinkle of that, this perfect partnership would have never occurred.

Since the duo has met with such great success, it's hard to believe that the earth didn't shake when George and Andrew met. In any case, you'd picture these elegantly clad young hipsters gracefully bumping into each other in the most glamorous circumstances. You can just imagine them meeting on a cruise, or in the gambling halls of Monte Carlo. Both are surrounded by gorgeous girls, but their eyes meet and they realize that an invincible friendship is possible . . . and so on.

Sorry to be disappointing, but George and Andrew met under decidedly different conditions. Let's go back, back in time, to mid-term at Bushey Meads High School. . . .

George landed at Bushey Meads at the tender age of twelve. He arrived part-way into the term, and, like any kid, he had a few problems adjusting. Latecomers usually have a hitch or two when they're thrown into a situation where everyone else has found a place. People who were nervous wrecks on the first day have scrambled around and settled into solid cliques. Some of them quickly forget how they felt that first day, and a newcomer can run into some tough situations.

Gorgeous George had a couple of additional strikes against him: he wore glasses and was a bit on the pudgy side. Sister Melanie credits his post-baby bulges to a bizarre eating habit: chomping down peanut butter and jelly sandwiches! "He hated school dinners," she explained, "so he'd take packaged peanut butter and jam sandwiches. Revolting! It was a habit he picked up from some American neighbors we had. No wonder he put on weight."

Obviously, English aren't big fans of that particular American delicacy. On the other hand, can you seriously picture yourself gulping down one of their lunchtime faves . . . "Toad in the Hole"? Probably not, even though it's not as gross as it sounds. (It's really a dish consisting of sausage encased in potatoes.)

Andrew had been a student at Bushey Meads for almost a year when George made his less-than-spectacular entrance. What George lacked in immediate impact, he made up for in sudden impact. He made an impression on Andrew that will never be forgotten.

"I don't actually remember him coming into class or anything," Andrew recalled in *Star Hits*, "but I remember at the time we were playing 'King of the Wall.' As he was the new boy, we goaded him into it. I was up there and he threw me off!! I was a mite peeved about this actually but I forgave him."

George recalled the results of the same spirited game: "... I threw him off and he hit his head. He was one of the rowdy ones in the class, so that was a major breakthrough. ... Everyone respected me after that ... until they realized it was a fluke."

That was the beginning of the odd couple. In those days, George was on the big side in height as well as weight. He must have seemed ungainly and awkward when compared to wiry Andrew. His large wire-frame glasses didn't hide the one bushy eyebrow that stretched across his forehead, and he had tons of uncontrollable curly hair to contend with. What a difference a few years can make!

Andrew is a completely opposite case. He's always been as downright delicious as he is today! However, he wasn't much in demand; devilish Andy walked too far on the wild side for most girls' taste. Girls could not keep up with him long enough to catch him.

It's a good thing that Andrew took care of his appearance. He's responsible for influencing ugly duckling George to aspire to swanhood. George saw how Andrew did things, and he tried to adapt them to himself. He got contact lenses and lost weight and today is one of the hunkiest swans in the flock.

Andrew is a perpetual peacock, and his "vanity" stretches back to grade school. His mom says that they never really fought very often about anything...except clothes. Unfortunately, a boy's good taste in his wardrobe isn't reflected in his school clothes when he's growing up in England. British boys and girls are almost always uniformed in the grade-school years. The kids at George and Andrew's school wore green blazers.

The terrible twosome wound up sitting next to each other in class. Andrew claims he suggested it, and George claims the teacher suggested it. Maybe she thought that George was the serious bookish type and set him next to the class swashbuckler to spread some "good influence" around. If that was the case, things didn't work out the way she planned.

The boys discovered that their common ground was about as far afield of the three R's as you could get. They shared a powerful interest in music. Both especially loved pop star Elton John, who was just beginning to find acceptance as a bona-fide superstar.

Despite his looks, George was anything but a bookworm. He and Andrew huddled in the back of the class and talked and talked. Their shared sense of humor created a very strong bond, and the bond ripened into friendship. Andrew has commented that great friendships consist of many elements. Similar interests can get one off the ground, but to keep it floating you need much more.

The boys clearly needed each other as much in their

school days as they do now. Their friendship is a well-balanced exchange, with a lot of give and take on both sides. Andrew helped George improve his appearance by example. He looked sharp and cool, and George couldn't help but want to look the same way himself.

George helped Andrew solidify his ambitions. Andrew had a certain amount of drive, but it was unfocused. He wanted to be famous, and he knew it. What he didn't know was if he wanted to be a football player, a musician, or King of the Wall! George, on the other hand, knew he really wanted to be a performer and singer, but didn't know exactly how to go about doing it. In Andrew he saw a chance to beat the odds and achieve his dream. Two heads are always better than one, especially when they're topped with two gorgeous faces!

When it came to football, George was not very interested. He has remarked that Andrew might have preferred to become a football star, because it was so much more masculine! According to George, it's a good thing that Andy picked music, because he wasn't as good at football as he thought he was. It's not that athletic Andy was any kind of slouch on the playing field; it's just that he might not have been the kind of exceptional player who becomes a sports superstar.

Two schoolboys with a lot of dreams . . . it almost sounds like the basic plot for a Broadway musical! The guys began seeing each other out of school, as well. They reviewed the weekly pop charts together and listened to the radio. English radio has always been excellent, and pop fans are treated to certain privileges that are unavailable to American audiences.

Until recently, people in Britain were much more interested in music than Americans. Because of the country's size, it doesn't take long for a record to spread to its entire potential audience. Nationalized radio stations covering the whole of Britain contribute to the speed with which a record can zip into popularity. These nationalized radio stations are owned by the government and divided into different audiences. "Radio One" is for pop music, and "Radio Two" is for adult contemporary and more middle-of-the-road music.

Since the charts change so rapidly, they're a lot more interesting to watch in England than in most American cities. To many British teens "chart day" is tremendously exciting. Everyone wants to know what went up and what went down. Artists who may have released only one single become stars almost overnight. After chart day, which is on Tuesdays, you can watch up-and-coming groups and other more established acts on the Thursday-night television show called "Top of the Pops." To get on this show, a single must have made it into the Top Forty.

Andrew Ridgeley and George Michael were mostly interested in established groups and singers, like Queen and Elton John. Most of us have heard of these famous folks, but one of the other bands they both liked is not so familiar. That band was called the Sweet.

The Sweet were an English "glitter" band. Americans didn't have very much of a glitter scene, but it was all the rage in England during the early to middle seventies. Performers like Gary Glitter and the Sweet influenced American rock stars like Joan Jett. Glitter music was very bouncy and sing-along–oriented, with heavy, crashing guitars and a big beat! (Many of the performers also dressed up outrageously.) It was good-time music, and the boys enjoyed it.

One of Andrew's first records was bought by his dad, Albert. It was a Sweet single called "Wig Wam Bam." Does that sound vaguely familiar? George admitted that "the closest I ever got to being a fan was when me and three other blokes adopted the names of the people in Sweet."

Comparing notes on your faves is a long way from actually doing anything yourself. It was going to be a long time before George and Andrew ever got on stage together, but it was well worth the wait. From the first moment they met it was practically destiny that they work together . . . forever.

FIRST STEPS
AND PARENTAL
PROBLEMS

The first time Shirley Holli-
man ever laid eyes on George Michael he was walking
from music class with his arm around something curvy.
No, it wasn't a girl. ... It was a violin! The people Shirley
hung out with teased George quite a lot for playing classical music. They were convinced that classical music was
for nerds only. Shirley would have laughed in your face
if you'd told her that in a few years George Michael would
make her a star.

Violin or no, neither of the guys fit into the typical
picture of nerd-dom. They would sign into the study hall
and then go running off to Andrew's house for a quick
educational session with the record player.

Listening can lead to less passive and more creative pursuits. George and Andrew were soon involved in a few tentative tryouts of their own. "George had a tape recorder at his house," Andrew reminisced, "we used to go over there and thrash things out on his drum kit and an old acoustic guitar."

The Wham! wonders got more experimental than that. They concocted their very own radio station! It was a very fun and creative idea. They taped songs from the radio and surrounded them with advertisements, chatter and phone-ins—whatever amused them and made an interesting combination. It was similar to collages you make in art class from bits of magazines, except it was a collage of sound.

The two had great times together, but every friendship can run into rocky ground, no matter how well the friends themselves get along. Interference often comes from outside the friendship itself, and George and Andrew had to face this problem on more than one occasion when they were growing up.

Lesley Michaels wasn't fond of her son's new best friend. Andrew even thinks she hated him, although he might be remembering things as being worse than they were. It certainly hurt his feelings, and George's too. It's never pleasant when your parents don't like your friends. You feel sad and uncomfortable, because you're caught in the middle. Emotions run high, making the whole thing difficult to talk over.

Maybe George's parents didn't trust his judgment, or maybe they were a little jealous because their loving son was spending so much time with another person. Maybe they were just concerned and protective, or temporarily thrown off by the surprise of discovering that George's new pal was so different from him. It could have been for any of these typical reasons.

Andrew's first visit to the Michael house occurred on George's birthday. Mrs. Michael had a mouth-watering tea made up, with lots of fruit and other nice morsels. The festive affair confused young Andrew, because everything looked bright and happy, but George's parents weren't happy with him. Lesley obviously didn't like him, and Jack wouldn't even speak to him.

One reason for their dislike was very clear to George. The Michaels thought Andrew distracted George from his schoolwork by encouraging and sharing his dreams of pop stardom. Actually, George was much more interested in music than Andrew was. "I think my parents thought it was all Andrew's fault that I wasn't concerned about school anymore," George explained in *Bop* magazine. "I don't think that they wanted to come to terms with the fact that it was my decision as much as Andrew's."

On the other hand, the Ridgeleys never really hindered Andrew's pursuits. Early on, they threw up their hands and gave up on getting the young roustabout Ridgeley interested in school. School was the last thing he found interesting, and that was that. Jenny Ridgeley is a schoolteacher herself, so dealing with that particular problem must have been very touch and go!

Luckily, this story has a happy ending. Many of these stories do. Eventually, kids and their parents get to the point where things can be worked out. For George and Andrew, that point was a few more years down the road.

EXECUTIVE SOUL

*D*ear Sharon,

   I'm writing this in math class. Want to do a friend
a big favor? Do a bit of spying for me and find out
if G.M. is seeing anyone. I can't believe how much
he's changed! 'Member when he slunk in here all
dumpy and dull? I thought he was such a jerk and
now I fancy him like mad. *I* might even ask him
out!!!! Hurry with info.

                                       luv, Debbie

   It's easy to imagine the kind of notes that began flying
between the girls at Bushey Mead when George started
shedding his shell. Quite a few changes were in store for

27

George and Andrew, and several advances were made into female territory.

George had his first crush when he was young, although he wasn't as young as Andrew was when he had his first crush! When he was six or seven he discovered the bittersweet pleasure of unrequited love when he fell for his math teacher. By the time he had his first date, when he was fourteen, he was in a much better position to show a girl how to paint the town red with something other than crayons!

For two months, he dated a girl named Lesley, a classmate. George looked grown-up enough to take his date out to London clubs. The Global Village and Cherry's were two of his hangouts.

George and Andrew had adopted their first real image. Now they were more than just a couple of guys who were into music—they were "Soul Boys." Soul Boys are an almost exclusively English phenomenon, though they exist in other parts of Europe in one way or another. They live to dance, and travel in groups to any venue that's willing to play their fave discs.

What did Soul Boys listen to? Besides Motown and other classic soul, George and Andrew were into artists like Sylvester and Chic. The first disco record George ever purchased was the brilliant "You Make Me Feel (Mighty Real)," by Sylvester. Soul Boys search for the ultimate big beat and brashest bass line. They need a soundtract to strut to, something that makes them feel bouncy and proud. Soul Boy music is music to look good to.

And Soul Boys spend a lot of time looking good. They wear sharp clothes and immaculate haircuts. Looking good is part of the fun and glamour. George enjoyed his new-found handsomeness, but he still had trouble forgetting his former days as a dumpy little boy. These memories still hinder him occasionally.

Andrew wasn't interested in a steady until he was seventeen or eighteen. He played the field with gusto in the tradition of most great playboys. Andrew's always been a charmer, and settling down with a girl was probably the furthest thing from this energetic teen's mind.

By this point you're probably wondering what kept Andrew and George from forming a band of their own. Was it the parental pressures? School? Football? Girls? Embarrassment or doubt? Indecision? An awful combination of earthquakes, tidal waves, and volcanic fury? Changing voices?

As usual, several forces including some of the above were at work. So if you think it strange that Wham! didn't immediately form the minute George and Andrew met, consider the following points.

People achieve their goals in different ways, with different circumstances surrounding them. In the crazy world of fame and fortune, the best-laid plans can fall apart and the wildest dreams can come true. It's a frightening prospect, being involved in an unpredictable business. When it came to actually getting the show-biz ball rolling, the boys disagreed.

Andrew wanted to form a band whenever George was ready, and the sooner the better! He thought that waiting until they were fourteen was cautious enough. George refused. He told Andrew that they would form a band after they finished O-levels.

In Britain, students face an examination system quite unlike the American one. O-levels are a primary test taken before age sixteen. You get them in different subjects, but you pick them according to what you intend to do after high school is finished. College is the next step up the ladder, if you choose. In college you study for A-levels, but you can also remain in high school to study for A-levels. English college isn't the same as American college; it's sort of a resting place between high school and university. Getting into university depends on your O and A levels.

A and O levels are used for more than determining what university you attend (if you go at all—most people don't). These tests qualify you for certain jobs. As you may have heard, unemployment is one of England's greatest problems. Getting a job is difficult, but getting a job without qualifications is almost impossible. Librarians need as many as five different O-levels, and good clerical jobs and business positions require even more.

You can see why these tests were important to George, and he convinced Andrew to wait a little longer. Andrew might not have been crazy about the idea (delaying the band for a bunch of tests indeed!), but he managed to pass quite a few O-levels himself . . . five in all! Three of them are in difficult subjects, like math, physics, and biology. The other two are in English and art. Andrew even went on to college, but not for the purpose of getting his A-levels. "I went there to escape having to go to work," he told *Smash Hits*. "It certainly wasn't a waste of time though. I think I learned more about things in general at college than I would have at school."

One thing Andy learned at college was how to appeal to the feminine section of the human race. This is when he first got a taste of heartthrob status. George agrees that Andrew's education wasn't book-related. Academics were out. . . . Being slick was in! Andrew was really thrilled with the idea of being "big man on campus." However, his interest in higher education did not quite extend to what he learned in class. After he'd made a dramatic entrance in the morning looking tasty, the thrill went downhill. He even dated to look good, George has recalled. "I remember he had this brief flirtation with this absolute dragon who was really trendy."

After O-levels, George had another reason to wait awhile before forming a band. He told Andrew that he wanted to finish his A-levels! Andrew was tired of waiting, and he got very insistent. He was so insistent that the boys' first real band, the Executive, formed that night. On November 5, 1979, Andrew and George took their first step to stardom.

EXECUTIVE EXIT

"I turned on her and told her that if she tried to stop me, I would leave school and home."
—George in *Me and My Mum*

*T*hese forceful words were spoken in desperation and anger. They don't sound like the kind of thing George Michael would fling at the mother he loves so much, but it happened. Once George had put aside his doubts, he was determined to put everything into the Executive. George's mom backed off after the argument; she had enough sense to know when her boy was deadly serious. It meant facing up to the fact that George would never be a lawyer, but sometimes mothers must learn that they cannot force their children to be something they don't want to be.

George Michael never needed a lot of training to be a first-rate singer/songwriter. The training he has isn't ac-

33

tual school training at all. George's skill as a musician
and arranger comes from two things. One of them is ability
to really listen to records that other people have put out.
When George listens to a song, he learns from it. He
absorbs parts of it and uses the select information to help
develop his own songs. He listens very carefully, so he
can be inspired by what others do without copying it.

George's other asset is his great talent (of course), but
his at-home, do-it-yourself training is essential too. When
it comes to book learning, George did an O-level in musical theory . . . but it isn't helpful to him these days. He
barely passed the test, and he can't remember a thing he
learned. George is no math whiz, and that's a prerequisite
in music theory.

It's interesting to take a peek at some of the changes
that influenced George and Andrew when they formed
the Executive. These influences are still with them today,
and they are one of the things that make Wham! special.

For starters, Andrew and George were isolated from
the hubbub and explosion that punk brought to Britain in
the mid-seventies. They were two middle-class suburban
boys who were happy with their basic surroundings. They
didn't feel a need to react in a particularly violent way.
Other people were very excited by punk, and they rushed
out to form their own bands. George and Andrew didn't
participate in the whirl of local bands that formed fast
and fell apart faster. They were still interested in the more
subtly flamboyant lifestyle of their Soul Boy friends.

Instead of going to concerts, George and Andrew went
out and danced. In a way, they were the stars of the show

when they hit the dance floor. George attended a couple of mainstream concerts; Elton John at Earl's Court was the first, in 1975. He also saw Queen, featuring firebrand Freddie Mercury. He was impressed, but he was more impressed with what was happening streetwise. He and Andrew danced and soaked up soul and funk. A record from this period of time that really hit home was by Smokey Robinson's old band, the Miracles. It's called "Love Machine," and you can hear Wham!'s version of it on their first album, *Fantastic*.

Everyone was so infatuated with punk, it was hard for George and Andrew to pinpoint what they wanted to do. Nonetheless, this was a very important period for the boys. Between 1978 and '79 they worked by listening to many different kinds of music and isolating the parts they liked best. That's why Wham! have always had a special sound despite their changes. They also spent some time getting better acquainted with their instruments, instead of rushing out to play them.

In 1979, soul and funk music went through a very big change. Several black singles became "crossover hits" by getting into other charts besides dance charts. Other artists hoped that they too could find success this way, and funk music began to lose some of its spiky rough edges. This new brand of soul didn't appeal to George and Andrew as much as the old one.

Other styles of music that caught their attention were mostly revival sounds, or nostalgia-oriented music. One of them was a mainstay of the Mods, who represented a specific sixties lifestyle in England popularized by the

early Who. Mods are still around in England, and the idea
has even spread to California. Mod-type music was influenced by quite a lot of different elements. George and
Andrew were more interested in the sources than the
mutations the music eventually went through to reach a
wider audience. Ska especially enjoyed a big resurgence
in England. Bands like the English Beat, Madness, and
the Specials were shaking up people's hips, feet, and brains.
The music is very energetic, with a kind of reggae beat
(it originated in the West Indies). The playing is simple,
but it requires mountains of vim and vigor.

The Executive mostly played other people's songs, or
"cover" songs. One was a ska version of "Can't Get Used
to Losing You" by Andy Williams. It must have been a
good idea, because someone else had it too: the song was
eventually covered by the English Beat, and it was a hit
for them.

The Executive consisted of George and Andrew and
two other guys from their school who had a yen for the
bright lights. But George and Andrew were so close already that they found it impossible to get into any kind
of permanent groove with the other members. A band is
built on cooperation and communication. A lack of either
breeds trouble with a capital T.

Speaking of which, they also had trouble with their
folks, and it was big trouble. George's father was absolutely opposed to the whole thing. George explained:
"You're surrounded by people who are trying hard and
failing dismally, and you've got to convince your parents
that you're not one of those people. They don't realize

the difference between a hit song and a bad song."

The Executive only lasted for five gigs, but it was enough to get George and Andy going. They played at the school disco, as most young bands do. They also played at a place called the Pump House in Watford, for a very appreciative audience. Melanie Michael remembers all the kids dancing along enthusiastically.

The boys still have memorabilia of the Executive hidden away somewhere. They find it rather humiliating now, but back then it was a good laugh. One of their fondest memories is of the time they played with some people who were to make it big in the British funk scene a few years down the pike.

"The funniest gig," Andrew told the NME, "was at my college. We had already gone on. . . . There was a band called Fizz, who Imagination were born out of. It was hysterical because they walked into this dressing room with big sunglasses . . . waltzing in with cashmere coats saying they'd just come off a tour in America."

"We just sat there behind this wall killing ourselves laughing," George chimed in. But things got even funnier at that Executive performance.

For instance, the other members of the band had engaged in a little mutiny. Missing in action were the bass player and guitarist. Oh, well, the boys figured, those are the breaks! They still had two days before the gig to learn the ropes. At the soundcheck, George finished learning his bass parts, or so he thought. He forgot them somewhere into the set. Great stars can always pull a rabbit out of the hat. George decided that if he couldn't play the lines, he could at least sing them. This worked rather well.

Andrew, who saw which way the wind was blowing, decided it was time to join in the hullabaloo. He ran into the dressing room and jumped back onstage dressed in Scottish clothes, including a kilt! Andrew was so excited about dancing around in his silly outfit that he forgot to sing most of his parts, but everyone ended up enjoying themselves.

The Executive got much further than one of George's other dreams. Sadly, he was forced to give up one of his early ambitions. Young George had leanings toward one of the professions that many boys find exciting; he wanted to be an airline pilot. Can you picture it? Captain George Michael, flying here and there . . . melting the hearts of countless stewardesses, passengers, and native girls! There would be a panic in the sky when they caught sight of him in his dashing uniform. It was a lovely dream, but George failed an eye test that was given by the school. Later he found out that he was partially color-blind.

George never really wanted any other "job." With his airborne hopes shot down, the Executive were proving that he'd picked the right path. The band attracted a decent amount of local attention. George and Andrew were even recognized by strangers occasionally, and they really seemed to be breaking ground. One of Britain's prestigious ska labels, Go-Feet, was interested in them.

It was especially rewarding that the label was primarily interested in George and Andrew's original compositions. "We were very pleased for a couple of weeks, but then the band broke up," George explained.

The communication problems had finally overtaken the Executive. After a few gigs and a minimum of recorded material, George and Andrew's first band was gone forever.

WIG WHAM!
BAM BAM

"One of the funniest things ever written about us was that we were the new Sonny and Cher. The worst thing was in our first ever interview in a music paper. I was quoted as saying 'we let others do the thinking for and about us.'"

—Andrew

George Michael and Andrew Ridgeley have come a long way, personally and professionally. Unlike most of us, Wham! grew up in public. The story of their journey from tenderfeet to top cats is chock full of ups, downs, and in-betweens.

First, we go back to Bushey. The Executive existed no more, and George and Andrew found themselves at square one again. They had some songs, piles of ambition, and each other. That's what they had. What they didn't have was a) a recording contract and b) decent steady jobs.

As mentioned, unemployment is very common in Britain, especially among kids just out of school. Many kids are left high and dry, although a few find the jobs they seek. These "lucky" ones often end up with tedious no-chance-of-advancement part-time jobs. Others live on supplementary benefits dispensed by the government, known as the dole. The government isn't exactly handing out massive amounts of money so kids can spend a couple of years on paid vacation. Dole kids usually end up with between seventeen and twenty-five pounds a week. If you're living at home, it can be okay. If you're not, rent benefits are available, but twenty-five pounds doesn't go very far when you have to pay for all your little expenses. It certainly doesn't leave anything left over for fun!

You've probably heard the dole mentioned often in interviews with English pop stars. Mostly they speak of the effect it has on the young people who are forced to "sign on." After a while, many of them become depressed and lethargic; they have nothing to do and no money to do it with. They want to break out of this vicious circle, but it seems impossible.

It takes ambition and spunk to bust out of the dole lifestyle. George and Andrew were determined to use their time, rather than fritter it away. The boys have explained that if they'd had steady jobs, there probably wouldn't be any Wham! today. It would have slowed down things considerably, and neither wanted that.

In those days, George worked at this and that. He had quite a few part-time jobs, including a stint as a cinema usher and occasional nights as a guest DJ. One night in that movie house proved to be worth millions of dollars. George was 17, and he'd been having some serious love problems. You see, he'd cheated on his girlfriend and she'd taken a powder. Sound familiar? Yes, it's the situation that inspired "Careless Whisper." George wrote it while he was ushering.

Andrew wasn't interested in getting some dead-end job, even to supplement his dole check. He saw the thing as more of a vacation than George did, but after a bit it even began getting on his nerves. Andrew's too active to settle into laziness, so he went out and looked for work. "He used to go to interviews and describe them to me afterwards," George remembered in *No. 1*. "It would have been so obvious that he didn't want the job that there's no way on earth he would have got it. To this day he would be unemployed."

The situation may have been bleak, but the boys kept their spirits up. During the day they worked on their songs and dreamed their dreams. George and Andrew knew that show biz was the only biz for them, and they weren't about to believe anyone who told them they were useless without a proper job. This philosophy was the word they spread with their very first single, "Wham! Rap." It helped pull them through these long days.

Andrew enjoyed waking up in the morning and going over to George's. As far as he was concerned, he *was* going to work. At night the boys and their little gang, including Shirley and David Austin, hit the clubs and dance floors in earnest. Hard funk was back with a vengeance, and they wanted to be out enjoying it.

Their nights out were bright even without loads of cash, but there were a few dark clouds on the home front. . . .

Jack and Lesley Michael were getting pretty upset with their growing boy. George showed no sign of abandoning his dreams, and as he got older he got more adamant about them. He was stuck on the idea of being a pop star. Jack and George argued frequently about everything associated with careers and music. Jack still wanted George to work toward what he thought of as a secure future.

To lighten the tension, George had to compromise. That's why he felt he had to work when Andrew didn't. As long as a bit of money was coming in, he couldn't be accused of terminal laziness.

Jack even told George not to buy any more albums, but George would sneak them in or tell his dad they belonged to someone else.

"There's one thing I learned," George commented in the *T.V. Times*, "if my children ever want to do anything ridiculous then I'll let them get on with it because stopping them makes them twice as strong."

Meanwhile, the boys did manage to get together a demo. It was finished in the early part of 1982, and it featured a little bit of each and the songs they'd been working on. Andrew and George were both very confident; they knew that someone would be interested in their youthful and energetic tunes.

Finally in February, they found an interested party. The snippets of "Come On," "Wham! Rap," "Club Tropicana," and other catchy Wham! songs had done the trick.

The company was called Innervisions, a small outfit run by a man named Mark Dean. In March, the boys were signed. Wham! were finally going to put out a record!

REACHING FOR
THE MOON

When the dashing duo de-
cided on the moniker "Wham!" they meant business.
Wham! is easy to remember. Wham! jumps out at you.
Wham! is short and sweet. Wham! means WOW!!! George
and Andrew slid around for a while, testing out Wham
Bam, Bam Wham, Wham Bam Bam . . . etc., but Wham!
was enough to get the message across.

So they had a name and a contract. The image came
naturally. What they didn't have was lots of money. The
Innervision contract may have given the boys a start, but
it wasn't a lucrative deal. Wham! was signed for about
three thousand dollars, and the money to be received from
royalties on record sales would be a very small percent-
age.

Undaunted, the guys went into the studio and emerged with "Wham! Rap (Enjoy What You Do)." The toetapping single died an unsightly death. Wham! couldn't believe it and were terribly hurt and distraught. It must have seemed like the end of the world. They were very upset with the record company. George and Andrew thought that Innervisions hadn't put enough work and promotion behind their debut release.

It was a rotten beginning, but things soon started looking up. Wham! presented the public with the fabulous "Young Guns." This time they responded.

As "Young Guns (Go For It)" began crawling up the Top 40, Wham! were invited to appear on "Top of the Pops." The boys, along with Shirley and Dee C. Lee, burst onto the television screens with a great beat and fast feet. They looked and sounded like stars, and their all-out entertainment really shone through the tube!

Not many groups have given their records such a terrific boost with one lone television appearance. And not many young groups even get on the charts with their second single. "Young Guns" Wham!ed up the chart and settled eventually in the number-four slot. The boys from Bushey were on their way to the top in earnest. This time the song's supposedly controversial nature helped them.

Controversial? Wham!? Isn't that more Frankie Goes to Hollywood–type territory? What were the boys saying to the British public back then? And why was it making them nervous?

"Wham! Rap" dealt with a subject that the people of Britain are not comfortable with: unemployment. The ones who suffer from it want it talked about more. The ones in charge don't want it talked about at all. Unfortunately, the in-chargers also rule the radio to a certain extent. "Wham! Rap" had limited airplay on the government-run BBC, so it only got to number ninety-one in the charts. With no television, limited airplay, and not enough attention from the record company, a single has nowhere to go but nowhere!

Luckily, "Young Guns" got the break it deserved. Some people found Wham!'s message to wedlocked teens offensive; they discovered all sorts of hidden meanings in the spirited rap. Most of these meanings were also hidden to George and Andrew, who had no idea what was going on. They were accused of being woman haters, homosexuals, and so on. People took sides. People argued. People bought the record to see what was being talked about. The talk might have been annoying to the boys, but they were glad that they were regarded as something worth talking about. It was important to them not to be seen as the "all haircut, no brains" variety of pop star.

Wham! did try to balance the scales with their television appearances. "Young Guns" wasn't meant as a totally serious song; it was a bit of a spoof. George, Andrew, and Shirley and Dee managed to get the irony across in their dancing and mugging. Soon people became familiar with the real Wham!, a fresh group with a fresh way of doing things.

Back in 1983, Wham! didn't play live shows. They laughed and danced and lip-synched their way through a number of personal appearances, but they weren't yet ready to get up onstage with a band. George and Andrew wanted everything to be right, and they weren't prepared to jump blindly into live work merely because it was expected of them.

Besides, there was an album to pull together, and that demanded enough of their attention. George was in a quandary trying to write a new single. In the meantime, Innervisions rereleased "Wham! Rap," which gave him a little breathing space.

"Bad Boys" came out in May 1983. Getting it out had been a long and dramatic ordeal, requiring three studios, months of hard work, and over ten thousand pounds! But the agony resulted in ecstasy for the boys when the single reached number two in June. "Bad Boys" even made a dent in the American charts by getting into the Top 100.

Wham!-mania was in full swing. "Bad Boys" came out of every radio, and streams of people poured their money in video jukeboxes to see Wham! sing, dance, and strut their stuff. The papers started writing of their trials and tribulations. Meanwhile, George and Andrew were getting their album together.

Fantastic was almost called "brilliant," but at the time there was a band floating around called Brilliant, and if they had called their album *Wham!*, there might have been mass confusion! Speculation aside, George and Andrew didn't want anyone to be the least mixed up about who they were, so they changed the title of their debut.

Whether the LP was fantastic or brilliant, it was slated for success. Wham!'s first album made chart history! *Fantastic* entered the British charts in the biggest way possible, straight in at number one. Only three or four other acts have achieved this instant success.

Three hit singles and a number-one LP spell out one thing to most people: living life in the fast lane. But Wham! weren't seeing any such spoils at this point.

The boys were under a lot of strain. Their deal with Innervision looked worse by the minute. Their records were selling, but their royalty deal pretty much excluded them from any real profits.

Innervision had problems of its own when it came to their newest, most formidable act. Innervision was a subsidiary of CBS. The bigger company controlled the smaller company's wallet, and the money to support Innervision acts was not flowing as loosely and freely as it should have. With a number-one album in the charts, Wham! were in a very bad position. They could not really afford to tour in the style that they wished, and they weren't ready to settle for second best.

Clearly something had to change. George and Andrew decided that they were in over their heads. They couldn't possibly fight this problem alone, so they began looking for a manager.

And luckily they found a terrific manager. Simon Napier-Bell's reputation usually comes into the room a few feet ahead of him. In the sixties, he managed the Yardbirds, the legendary white blues group that spawned guitar greats Jimmy Page, Jeff Beck, and Eric Clapton. He has also steered the careers of the British group Japan, and the very influential and much-missed Marc Bolan of T-Rex.

Simon Napier-Bell has helped Wham! in many different ways over the years, but back in 1983 he needed to do two things right away. He had to get Wham! out on tour to support their album, and he had to get them released from their Innervision contract.

The tour was the easy part. In England and America, it's now common for various hip-minded companies to sponsor bands in exchange for their advertising time. Over here Lionel Richie and even the Jacksons have taken advantage of this kind of deal. The companies may ask for television time, or they may ask for some advertising space on the programs. When Fila sportswear decided to sponsor Wham! they asked the boys to wear their product onstage.

The tour was dubbed "Club Fantastic" and Fila very willingly bestowed fifty thousand pounds on the Wham! organization to get it rolling. And roll it did, right over Britain, leaving a trail of screaming and ecstatic fans behind it.

"Club Fantastic" opened up with a real club atmosphere. Wham! wanted to present their fans with more of the all-over entertainment that they'd seen and loved on that first "Top of the Pops" appearance.

Entertainment is what the fans got. George and Andrew had worked very hard solidifying Wham!'s sound. For months their lives revolved around what was happening in the studio. George pulled it all together with a marathon forty-eight-hour mixing session, and he and Andrew hit the stage with months of pent-up energy spurring them on. It's no wonder the audience was too excited to sit in its seats.

Fantastic was very important to the guys, and they wanted the tour to be just as special and original. Instead

WHAM!

Andrew and George go for a spin in a different kind of convertible.

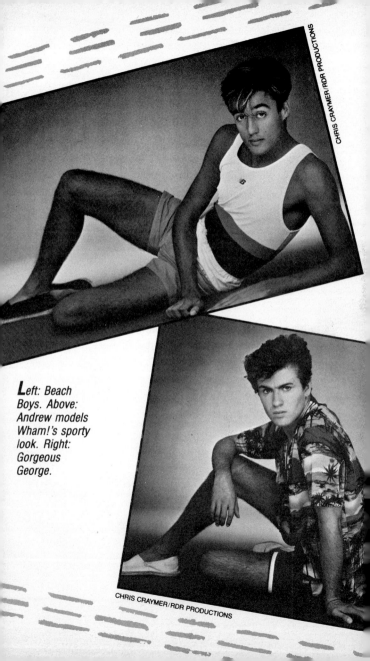

*L*eft: Beach
Boys. Above:
Andrew models
Wham!'s sporty
look. Right:
Gorgeous
George.

Right: Slick sounds from "Club Tropicana." *Below:* George shows us what he's made of.

ALLAN BALLARD/SCOPE FEATURES/RDR PRODUCTIONS

ALLAN BALLARD/SCOPE FEATURES/RDR PRODUCTION

*A*bove: Fun in the sun.

An intense moment with two superstars.

MICHAEL PUTLAND/RETNA LTD.

Below: Together forever as good guys and bad boys!

WHAM!
MAKE IT BIG

*L*eft above: request time? Left below: A Wham! party is always the hottest ticket in town.

*R*ight: Making it big onstage.

GENE SHAW/STAR FILE

*T*all, dark, and
handsome!

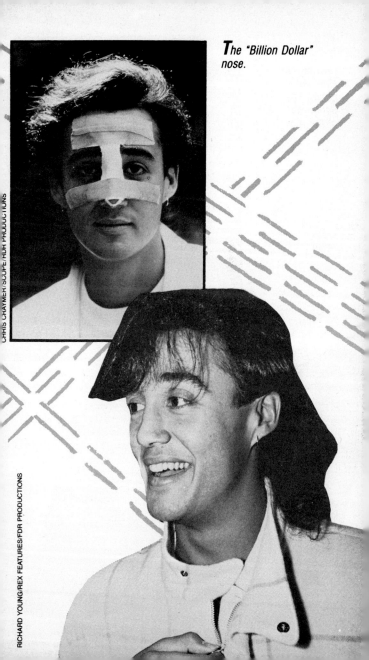

The "Billion Dollar" nose.

*R*ight: Proud George with Elton John. Below: The Songwriter of the year.

RICHARD YOUNG/REX FEATURES/RDR PRODUCTIONS

*L*eft: George and Andrew make a splash at the Ivor Novello Awards and—(below)— share a special moment at the Apollo theater during "Motown Returns to the Apollo."

*A*n unforgettable portrait
of two unforgettable guys.

NOM/RETNA LTD.

of toting around the usual opening act, Wham! took along a single friend. DJ Gary Crowley de-iced the crowd with his chatter and his platters. He spun some great dance tunes and got them wiggling their feet.

In the intermission, Wham! showed some movies. It was quite a break away from their well-organized videos. These were a combination of Mr. Ridgeley Sr.'s home movies of the boys when they were younger and various other unpretentious bits of historic and autobiographical Wham! footage.

The tour was a big success, despite George's small bout with a throat ailment. But what waited for Wham! at the end of the "Club Fantastic" was . . .

LEGAL
DIFFICULTIES

Suddenly Wham! were off the stage and spending a lot of time in courts. Not tennis courts but real, live legal courts. George and Andrew still wanted to be released from their contract with Innervision. In addition they had a brand-new problem. Another band had preceded them in using that name in the United States.

The American Wham had evidently discovered the British Wham! when George and Andrew visited the States for promotional purposes. The American Wham decided to sue, then eventually settled the case and Wham! had the right to use their name. During the lawsuit and other court maneuvers, the boys were required to stick the letters U.K. after their moniker.

Those two little letters were easy enough to lose, but the contractual mess was sticking like glue. One of the problems with their contract was pretty major. Wham! were supposedly not getting royalties from any of the twelve-inch singles they had released. As you can imagine, this did not exactly make them jump for joy. The boys from Bushey had gotten themselves into real trouble this time.

"Club Tropicana" had maintained the group's end of the bargain; it was a big hit. Now they wanted to see some of the rewards they deserved.

Wham! claimed that Innervision had used "undue influence" to get them to sign the contract. Innervision replied that it had spent over £120,000 on Wham! and it didn't want them recording for any other label.

For the whole winter, the warring factions pulled back and forth. During this time Innervision released the "Club Fantastic Megamix," which Wham! disowned on the English rock television show *The Tube*. They asked the fans not to buy it, and some of them listened. The disc only made it to number fifteen on the charts.

After what seemed like ages, Simon Napier-Bell fixed things by talking to Innervision's parent company, CBS. The band had lost its case in court, because the contract they signed, like it or not, was legal. CBS agreed to sign Wham! for a much better deal, but Wham! had to pay off Innervision first. When the dust settled, George and Andrew were right back where they started—almost.

A BRAND-NEW
WHAM!

Somewhere between sportswear city and the "Club Tropicana," Wham! shed their "big bad boys" image. What made them change? Were they tired of their usual "uniform" of black leather jackets, white T-shirts, and tight, ankle-cropped blue jeans?

The answer's simple: the boys had been play-acting. Of course they weren't really teenage hoodlums. They'd taken their idea as far as they wanted to, and it was time to develop a new concept. "The 'Bad Boys' image amused us to a certain degree," George explained. "The rebel image is always attractive. You can have a lot of fun playing someone who isn't yourself when you're on-stage."

Unlike some other groups, who become slaves to their image, Wham! was determined to be flexible and move with the times. George and Andrew had insisted that their tough-guy swaggering wasn't very serious, and now they proved it by dressing their healthy good looks in more suitable garb. Out went the blue jeans and leather jackets.

George had other reasons for wanting to abandon the studs 'n' stuff for suits and suntans: "I really don't like 'Bad Boys' in retrospect. I had to write a song to match up with some kind of rebellious aspect, which distracted from the music, I thought."

The change of style also reflected their changing lives. They were no longer two kids fresh off the dole; they were on the verge of becoming international stars. "We did our little bit of social stuff with 'Wham! Rap,'" George commented, "because that was our situation at the time. Now there's no point in pretending that I don't have everything I want."

A WEEKEND WITH WHAM!

What was that? A weekend with Wham!? Now where should we go? Bushey? Nahhh ... it would be nice to meet the folks and all, but Bushey isn't exactly a happening burg. Besides, England is too rainy this time of year, or any other time of year. How about France, then, romantic Paris or the exotic Riviera? What a great idea. It might look pretty impossible, but it isn't. This dream actually came true in glorious 3-D for a girl quite similar to any devoted Wham! fan. Her name is Debbie, and she was sent to France by *No. 1*, a top British pop magazine.

Actually, the phrase "number one" is a perfect all-around description of the occasion. The duo were re-

cording their future number-one album, *Make It Big*, in
the number-one country for luxury and romance. It goes
without saying that Wham! are number one on all of our
lists.

Let's drop in on the party and learn a little about what
happens when Wham! go to work.

The studio we're visiting is in Brignole, which is located near the southern coast of France. Brignole itself
has made it big in the wine business. In fact, it's in the
top five of France's wine-producing areas.

Debbie also comes from a coastal town, the British
seaside resort of Brighton in southern England. Brighton
is like a cross between Atlantic City without the intense
glamour and Coney Island without the intense grit of New
York City. It's a very pleasant place, but it couldn't compare to the grandeur of the Chateau Minerval, where the
recording studio is housed. The Chateau has hosted a
mixed bag of talents: Duran Duran, Yes, and old-timers
Pink Floyd, for instance. The next group to be penciled
in after Wham! was the Thompson Twins.

If seeing the Chateau for the first time was imposing,
you can imagine what it must feel like coming face to face
with Mr. George Michael for the first time. Anyone in
Wham!-dom would be a bit nervous . . . but when Debbie
meets George, she discovers that there isn't much to be
nervous about. He's just too sweet and cuddly to leave
a nice girl quaking in her boots for long!

Artists enjoy having their friends drop by and see them
when they are recording. It's a great opportunity to get
an outsider's opinion of the work you've been doing.
Debbie, photographer Chris Craymer, and writer Paul

Bursche have the pleasure of being some of the first people to hear Wham!'s efforts.

Visitors also get to hear recordings that never get released on a wide scale, like the "Working Man's Club" version of "Careless Whisper." It was done by a few of the crew in the studio one evening, and it turned out quite funny. We don't really have working men's clubs over here, but in England they are an institution. These clubs cater to the average guy; they are leisure centers for blue-collar workers. Your average guy singing the poignant "Careless Whisper"? It probably sounded more like a battle than a ballad!

George proudly displays the rest of Wham!'s new material to his guests. When met with unconditional approval, he beams as expansively as a first-time father. George's work is really important to him, and this devotion is even more obvious than usual when he's in the studio. He has something to be proud of; the *Make It Big* album contains the best Wham! ever committed to vinyl ... yet.

During the recording sessions, Andrew is more at liberty than George, especially because George has more than one job this time. A little liberty is fun, but a lot of liberty can be a dangerous thing. Sometimes all that freedom isn't for the best, and even wild and imaginative Andrew is having trouble making his own fun. Not much is hopping around the Chateau, except maybe a few frogs, and the boys have already been there for five weeks.

People who aren't in the music business often picture studio sessions as one huge party. Sure, artists have fun at these sessions; it's one of the few jobs in the world where whistling while you work is essential! It's a very intimate and "in" kind of atmosphere, and when you see glimpses of it on television, it looks like the ultimate in excitement and hotshot pizzazz.

The secret that the artists keep from you is that more often it's the ultimate in exhaustion and cold pizza. Making a record is a long, complicated process, where (usually) each instrument is recorded one by one, the singers add their voices on top of that, and then all the different tracks are put together in a "mix."

It's fortunate that we're visiting the recording studio with Debbie. Through her we can see a little of what life is like behind the mixing desk. It's a real blast to "hang out with the pros" for a couple of days, even if it's only on paper; but a couple of days isn't the same as a couple of months.

The control booths of studios are full of bright lights and bright ideas. This is where things really happen. All the important machinery is located here, and this is where the action is. Control booths are usually small, if not downright tiny. The equipment has to be stored efficiently for easy access. Otherwise the producer and engineers would spend most of their time walking back and forth.

Sitting in a weeny little room for hours and hours staring at winking lights may not sound terribly taxing to you, but consider it this way: it's the kind of thing they train astronauts to do! Like astronauts, studio personnel and artists must make many important on-the-spot decisions, and mistakes can cost thousands of dollars.

The payoff for this claustrophobia and weeks of long hours and hard work is a record that sounds fantastic and sells like hotcakes. No artist would deny that the payoff is worth every minute of struggle in the studio.

In between the nerve-wracking mental pressures, there's a lot of waiting. Have you ever spent a whole day waiting for one thing after another? It can be very draining. If you're just waiting for one thing to happen, at least you feel tremendous relief when it's over. But when you have to wait in one line, and then another, and the rest of your day is taken up with waiting for various people to call or stop by, then it becomes the longest and most frustrating day in the world!

All this tension in a close space can create big problems for George, Andrew, and their coworkers. After a while the effect is similar to cabin fever, a condition where people get crazy from being locked up together for too long. Fights can start out of nothing, which is why a lot of less together bands have split up in the studio. In any case, these fights have to be avoided if possible, because unhappy people can't make truly happy music.

Naturally, Wham! have it better than hundreds of other groups. They get to record in better surroundings, and their friendship is rock-solid enough to last through the tiffs. They're a fine example of how real friendship can transcend any obstacle, even boredom.

Even the biggest, loveliest, and most well-equipped chateau can become boring in these situations. The fun of being in a new place and poking in all the new nooks and crannies fades when it starts to feel like your second home. The Wham! guys knew when they first began that no matter how famous and successful you are, there are still bad times and dull times and a job to be done.

What's to wait for at the Chateau Minerval? Plenty! Suppose George and Andrew decide that a special musician is needed for a track. They are very excited about getting the guest in to lay down his part, because they're thrilled by the idea they have. If the guy has previous commitments, it gets put off; when he finally arrives, a vital piece of equipment breaks down and it's time for everybody to moan and pull their hair out.

Faulty equipment is one of recording's biggest headaches. The machines used are delicate and break easily. One of George's problems when he is producing *Make It Big* is a glitch in a speaker.

The "acoustics" are minutely controlled in recording studios. "Acoustics" is the term artists and producers use to describe the sound quality of a specific room. The artist is looking for the best sound quality possible, because these tracks will be heard on every kind of system. A good-quality recording sounds great on both big disco systems and tiny car stereos.

If one of the speakers is sending out the wrong sounds, it can mess things up something fierce. When George mixes the collected instrumental and vocal tracks, he uses the desk to add tones and effects. So if a speaker is making a track sound tinny when it really isn't, he might level it by turning up bass tone. Then when the song is played on a speaker that isn't broken it would sound awful.

In this case, nothing can be done to fix the problem. Work has to be halted while a British expert is sent for.

Unexpected diversions are a welcome break in the routine of studio life. During the recording of *Make It Big*, Derek Warwick, a race car driver, drops in for a visit. He came to be shown around by the studio's owner, who is one of France's most famous jazz pianists. Eventually, Andrew gets hold of him for some serious car talk.

You can imagine how glad Andrew was to see Derek. He's always glad to meet people who share his interests, and after weeks of nothing but music, a change was appreciated.

This evening, George and Andrew decide to venture down to the town of Brignole for fun and feasting with their guests. A simple-enough wish indeed, but Brignole's supply of fabulous eateries is limited. In fact, it's limited to one.

Many of the best studios are located in quiet, secluded spots. Here the artists can have some privacy. The people in the surrounding village are usually not big rock fans, with little interest in the stars who regularly invade their territory. The stars themselves don't mind this. They can move about town freely, without the hindrances they usually face in other places (like fans chasing them all over the place!).

This night, Brignole's best is filled to the brim. Does George or Andrew cause a terrific scene and demand to be let in? No way—the boys and party adjourn to a less delectable establishment and make up for what the food lacks with cheery conversation!

The next day it is time for Debbie to go home. The boys kiss her farewell and present her with autographed souvenir bottles of the wine produced by the Chateau. With promises of an advance copy of the LP, Debbie wistfully whizzes away from her wonderful weekend with Wham!

Afterward, Debbie has nothing but good things to say about the boys. "They're really charming," she tells *No. 1*. "George is the one who's definitely in control, but I don't think he'd do anything without Andrew agreeing. They weren't like I expected at all. They're really down-to-earth and nice. George seems a little shy when you first meet him. But Andrew's fun from the first second. They're lovely!!"

ARE YOU READY TO WHAM!?

*I*n June of 1984, Wham! reappeared on the scene in Britain. They were brown from the sun, blond in the hair, and raring to go. They proudly declared that their new single would be an instant number one, but George and Andrew were a shade off in their calculations. "Wake Me Up..." entered the charts at number four and hopped to number one from there.

George and Andrew didn't mind the short delay. They'd been waiting years for a number-one single, and another week or two wasn't going to put them off. When the big day finally came, Wham! wore their hearts on their chests; the T-shirts they put on for their "Top of the Pops" appearance declared that they were really "NUMBER ONE"!

People were rather shocked by Wham!'s musical turn-around. "Wake Me Up Before You Go-Go" is a far cry from the tunes on *Fantastic*. Even "Club Tropicana" didn't come close to the lighter-than-air pop perfection of the new Wham! sound. George insisted that the new sound of Wham! was the real sound of Wham!. "I decided to write from instinct rather than demand and that's why the songs changed."

In August, George and Andrew caused more confusion. George released a solo single titled "Careless Whisper." The usual rumors of a break-up circulated, and the boys squashed them promptly and stylishly. George explained that the song didn't fit into the Wham! picture. The new Wham! was extra-snappy and springy, and "Careless Whisper" was the exact opposite. The idea seemed even more peculiar when it came to light that Andrew had helped compose the tune.

With two British number ones behind them, George and Andrew decided to go for one more to grow on. For weeks, England whistled along to the fabulous sounds of "Freedom" as they watched it become Wham!'s third number-one single in a row.

Wham!'s seasonal gift to their fans was a double A-sided single, pairing "Last Christmas" with "Everything She Wants." This combination platter never got further than number two in the British charts, and for once George and Andrew didn't want it to edge the current number one out of its slot. That was because the number-one single at the time was BandAid's "Do They Know It's Christmas?"

George and Andrew had participated in this historic

event, but they wanted to do more for the starving in Africa. The duo generously contributed all their royalties from "Last Christmas" to the cause, and their touching gesture set a wonderful example.

Naturally the second album, *Make It Big*, lived up to its title with a vengeance. The darling duo had chalked up yet another number one. Where could they go from here? Why, across the sea, of course. Wham! were finally ready for America. As it turned out, America was more than ready for Wham!.

WHAT DOES ANDREW FROM WHAM! DO?

When the press realized that Mr. Ridgeley did not write or contribute a bunch of fancy finger work to Wham!'s records, they became suspicious. All of a sudden, everyone wanted to know what the heck the other half of Wham! did to earn his keep. George painstakingly explained that Andrew's contribution to Wham! is substantial even though it's not obvious.

Andrew has been many things in the context of the group. At first he was George's inspiration when he wrote lyrics. Most of the songs on *Fantastic* are directed by Andrew in one way or another. When George wrote, he wanted to communicate with other young people. Andrew's sense of humor and outlook helped him to do this in a fresh and original fashion.

George insists that without Andrew, there would be no
Wham! George himself would have been a totally different
person if he hadn't met Andrew. Anyone who's had the
pleasure of seeing Wham! live knows that George just
wouldn't be such an exciting performer without his companion. Andrew's combination of interplay with his own
stage antics make for a very exciting evening.

The eighties' answer to Butch Cassidy and the Sund-
ance Kid have a very special friendship, and this friendship is what Wham! is based on. The great team had some
definitive words to say about the cynical reception Andrew had received, but they really summed it up in *Smash
Hits*:

When asked what Andrew's position in the group was,
George replied, "... That question's so boring. ... Why
does it matter? If you're making good records—and as
far as we're concerned we are—why does it matter?"

"All people see is us on 'Top of the Pops' and a few
pictures in the papers," Andrew added. "They don't realize about everything else that goes into making a career.
Intangible things. No one can define creativity. If you
don't have it, you can't be expected to understand it."

Surely that retort stung a few inquisitive ears. As Wham!
hoped, their explanations were eventually accepted. Finally the critics are beginning to understand something
that Wham! and their fans have known for a long time.

WHAM!, WOMEN, AND SONG

Wham! and women? What a perfect combination! George and Andrew think so, and they both love to spend lots of time in the company of the "fair" sex. What kinds of girls do they like? What do they like to do on a date? Do they ever fight over female attention? What's the real story?

When it comes to Wham!'s taste in girls, there is no "they." The boys have completely different tastes. What Andrew finds attractive isn't necessarily what George finds attractive.

George admits that there's one big obstacle standing between him and true love: his work. He's afraid of a serious commitment right now, because he's just beginning to achieve his goals. In his present situation, both parties could get hurt, and George doesn't want to hurt *anyone*!

True love is something that everyone is looking for, and George hopes that when he meets his perfect mate, he'll be able to give the relationship the attention it needs to thrive. George wants someone to share with, but he's not that keen on marriage right now. Then again, how many boys in their early twenties are? As it is, he barely has the time to date.

What kind of girl is George looking for? Someone who's intelligent and amusing. The all-important sense of humor that he shares with Andrew would have to extend into his love life for George to be really happy. As far as looks are concerned, George prefers women with a few curves. He's not enamored of wraithlike females. "I can't bear the thought of all those bones sticking in me," George has declared.

If you get the idea that George is a real bronco when it comes to chasing girls, then you're not quite on the mark. George did go through a phase where he dated a lot of different girls, but that was before he got famous. Back then, Wham! were just beginning to succeed, and the fun of getting to know as many girls as possible was a fresh experience.

So George went for the flattering attention, and he found out a few things. First, he discovered that he was still a bit shadowed by his old, unattractive self. He didn't have the confidence to be totally carefree and aggressive. Second, as he became more well-known, he discovered something much more disturbing. Suddenly, he wasn't

George the individual; he was George Michael, the prize! Women wanted to be seen with him and be with him because of his status, not because they liked him. George told *Tiger Beat Star*, "I hate the idea of being chased or abused, to think of girls telling their friends 'this will be a good one to tell' is horrible, and it has happened to me."

You can bet that Mr. George Michael is not interested in girls who are interested in him as a public figure. Perhaps that's why you don't hear much about the women George dates. Does George have anyone special in his life now? The answer is "yes" and "no." George is seen quite often with a young woman named Pat Fernandez.

George describes Pat as his "personal adviser, chocolate buyer and mascot holder." He doesn't really discuss Pat with the press, because she doesn't want him to. Pat is willing to talk about George, however, and laughingly told a *Smash Hits* reporter that George is "a lovely boy ... warm and tender ... but he was much more intelligent when he had brown hair." Pat is just teasing, of course. A lot of joking goes on between the two, but it seems that Pat could be either a girlfriend or a non-romantically involved companion. Either way, it's great that such a pleasant and sincere girl is in charge of purchasing George's sweets and looking after him.

Mostly, George needs someone who'll support him emotionally when the going gets tough. He needs a hardy woman who will help share the load. Even if it's just a matter of lending a sympathetic ear. In his line of work, George needs all the support he can get.

Miss Right may not be looming on the horizon, but George is in no hurry. While he has the love of his family and friends, George doesn't feel the need to cure loneliness with a quick forward dash into the first pair of open arms he sees.

Andrew makes up for George's sedate approach; he's armed with charm, he's smooth, he's slick, and he's had practice! Those liquid sultry eyes and stunning good looks knock roomfuls of eligible women off their feet. Andrew Ridgeley is a certified lady killer on the loose, and he isn't ashamed to admit that women are on his "A" list of priorities.

Put Andrew among a batch of attractive and lively girls and you'll have to protect your ears from the sonic boom he'll leave behind as he rushes toward them. This guy ain't shy!

"I'm infatuated with women," Andrew stated in *The News of the World Sunday Magazine*. "I absolutely adore women. It might be the young buck phase, but so what? ... I have no intention of cooling down." How's that for unconditional surrender?

Andrew goes for the tall and slim type, and when he finds them, one of his favorite activities is kissing. He isn't attracted to girls who bury their features under tons of cosmetics, and he's definitely not interested in the baggy-clothes brigade. Andrew prefers feminine females, in well-fitting skirts and dresses.

Dating Andrew can get pretty hectic. He likes to go out and have a riotous time on the town, so his datemates need loads of energy and perhaps a spare pair of hose to get through the night unscathed. It would also serve them well to remember that Andrew is an active girl-watcher.

He can't resist looking, and a jealous display will do more harm than good.

All tearing around aside for the moment, Andrew is interested in the more steady sort of love. "I love the idea of romance. . . . Without that there is no scope to develop a relationship . . . and I would like a real relationship," he confided in *Tiger Beat Star*.

Andrew's reasons for not settling down coincide somewhat with George's. This popular young man is far too busy to hold up his end of an important romance.

Andrew is very sincere about his desire to eventually quit the wild life . . . but he's not desperately seeking a soul mate. "I'm unattached and intend to stay that way for some time yet," Andrew affirmed in *Bop*. "Actually I don't think I've ever been in love and I have no desire to rush into marriage. George and I don't have normal jobs with normal schedules and we are always all over the place. So we never really get the time to find out what a girl's personality is really like."

That could be quite a problem when you're talking about things like serious commitments. Otherwise, Andrew just settles for getting to know his companions as well as possible in the short time allotted. Some people think he gets to know them a little too well, and that's where Andrew's reputation as a ladies' man comes from.

Like a lot of boys, Andrew likes to talk about girls. Occasionally he says things in fun that are taken way too seriously, but again that's one of the dangers of being famous! So, once in a while, Andrew gets into trouble.

You may have heard rumors about Andrew's devil-may-care lifestyle, but you may never have found their origin. In Britain, Wham! are nationally known celebrities. Kids, mums, dads, and grandparents all know the boys by sight. Whenever they get up to anything, good or bad, they make the front pages of the newspapers!

One of these episodes occurred in Bristol, and it made the front of the papers for several days before the boys left for China. Andrew attended a party at Bristol's Dragonara Hotel for a rugby club. He got a little tipsy, and several pictures were published of Andrew having a *very* good time. At some point in the evening, a jealous boy noticed that his girlfriend was missing—and so was Andrew Ridgeley. He added to the pandemonium by jumping to conclusions and bursting into a rage. In the throes of his anger, he supposedly bashed down a door with a fire extinguisher.

Sounds pretty over the top, doesn't it? The papers carried many more anecdotes concerning Andrew's alleged behavior. The next day a Wham! spokesperson stated, "Andy doesn't want to talk to the press, but this story is total fabrication. I know Andy, and this doesn't sound like him".

Poor Andy must have felt that his "fun" image was getting out of control. It was one reason for his press-shy attitude in China. George told *The Sun*, "Andrew was upset about the bad publicity he had in Bristol. It was just a typical night out for him. But it was all over the papers. It's not surprising he is now choked off with the press." When asked how he felt about Andrew's night out, George replied, "It's not my place to tell Andrew how to behave.... We understand each other and give each other space."

It's fantastic that Andrew's wonderful Wham! partner doesn't judge or condemn him. George knows that some of these love-life stories get quite silly and the least little thing can set off all sorts of gossip. Andrew told reporters as the duo flew to Hong Kong that George had fallen madly in love with Madonna... and they jumped all over it! George may admire the feisty American singer, but he's never exactly come out and declared undying love for her! Andrew may or may not have been having his little joke, but nothing's been said about Madonna since.

Another story concerned Andrew and two girls. Supposedly, two girls were waiting for Andrew when his American tour ended and they were threatening each other. Jackie St. Claire told *The Sun*, "If Andy ditches me for Elisha, I'll break his nose and give her a black eye." And Elisha coolly replied, "They've only got a sex thing, we've got something more."

A few days later, the girls appeared together in *The Sun* together wearing boxing gloves and not very much else. Most Wham! fans were on the floor when they saw this. The two beautiful girls were squaring off for Andrew's affections, and he hadn't even dropped so much as a comment about either one!

What a funny life the boys must lead. Imagine picking up the paper and reading something like that about yourself. That's show biz!

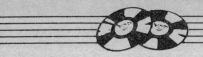

THE CHINESE CONNECTION

*T*wo bright young stars stride purposely through one of London's biggest airports. Photographers pop their flashes off in rapid succession, trying to capture the moment for hundreds of thousands of fans. The bright lights bounce off one of the guy's shiny blond-streaked hair, while the other shields his eyes with a pair of fashionable shades. They both rival the photographers with lightning flashes of their own; those two brilliant smiles could only belong to Wham!. They've been through many airports, posed for countless pictures, and made hundreds of appearances, but today is something special. Today Wham! is making history.

Wham! is about to become the first popular Western

music group to play in mainland China. They have been preceded only by Jean-Michael Jarre and a group called Morning Rise. Jean-Michael Jarre's electronic compositions are not widely known outside of France. Morning Rise was a group from California who played a few small select shows a year after Jarre.

Since Jarre opened things up a little in 1981, various superstars have been clamoring to be let in. Wham!'s idol Elton John managed to perform in Russia, but China wasn't ready for him. The Rolling Stones failed as well, along with Rod Stewart and the Police.

In Chinese, Wham! can be translated as "Wei Meing," meaning mighty and vigorous, and those words certainly describe the impact that the Wham! extravaganza had on the Chinese officials who attended a show in Japan. The concert was a sell-out, of course, and the investigating committee was impressed by what it saw. They asked for some more material on the band, and the wheels that would roll Andrew and George all the way to the Far East were set in motion.

A Wham! representative commented on the officials' reaction: "They thoroughly enjoyed it. The only thing they were worried about was the volume. . . . Afterwards they checked all the lyrics and records to see if it was suitable for their population" (*The Star*, March 5).

Wham! needing the Chinese government's stamp of approval to play their 100% Grade A music may sound a little strange, but then life in China is not at all like life in the Western world.

Chinese life is based on the economic system of communism. Like capitalism, which is our economic system, communism comes in many different forms. For instance, if you went to Japan you would see the Japanese form of capitalism. There are very big differences between Russian and Chinese communism. In China they have been very strict about letting in Western influence. Things are done communally, for the good of the group, and the Chinese are wary of anything that puts the individual before the group. Western stars, on the other hand, are clearly individuals who are very different from the rest of the population. For one thing, they earn more money than the average person. In China, almost everyone earns approximately the same amount of money a week. A seamstress, for example, may earn as much as a doctor! China's leading songstress, a girl in her early twenties named Sing Fong Yuen, sells two million copies of every cassette she puts out. Her average salary is fifteen dollars a week! This may sound ridiculous to you, but it's a little more than most people in China make.

Another factor is the Chinese position on premarital hanky-panky—they're definitely against it! The government is very careful when it comes to protecting their youth from amorous ideas. When Wham! sent a selection of video shorts for final approval, they removed "Love Machine," because it might've been a little too hot for the Chinese to handle. Likewise, several scenes were cut from promo videos.

Wham! were then judged fit for Chinese consumption. Their sponsors (you need a sponsor to play in China, even if you're an orchestra), the All-China Youth Federation, which is an organization along the lines of Boy Scouts or Girl Scouts, would not all be in attendance when the group came to play. The Federation has somewhere over 200 million members!

Everyone was optimistic about the forthcoming expedition. "George and Andrew are delighted," enthused a Wham! representative in *The Star*. "I think they will go down the same as anywhere else—absolutely wonderfully."

Meanwhile in China, five different versions of George Michael's solo single, "Careless Whisper," have been recorded by Chinese artists. Most of them are in the Cantonese dialect, but one's in the Mandarin dialect. Everything has to be redone from scratch, because Western pop music isn't available over-the-counter in China. All this is changing because of Wham!, who is releasing two cassette packages on the only record company in town, the state-owned China Records. It isn't clear yet how the high finance will work out. Chinese artists don't receive royalties, and money is not allowed to leave the country.

When the situation is resolved, the boys will get some rewards for their cassette releases. One is a compilation, or greatest-hits–type package. The other is a five-track offering with Sing Fong Yuen on the other side. Wham! will be the very first Western pop group to have its records manufactured and released in mainland China, a land where one third of the population is between 12 and 25 years old! That's a lot of potential Wham! fans!

After two preliminary shows in Hong Kong, Wham!

was scheduled to fly to China. They had no idea what to expect, but some of the things that happened during the trip went beyond their wildest guesses.

WHAM!'S CHINESE TOUR DE FAB

Wham! didn't really get to "tour" China in the grand sense of the word. Their actual dates were limited to two—one at the twelve-thousand-seat People's Gymnasium in Peking, and one in Canton at the five-thousand-seat Zhingsham Memorial Hall.

The Chinese organizers were a bit unsure how people would react to the glittering duo's debut, so a longer tour wasn't approved. Martin Lewis, who produced the Chinese documentary of the visit, offered another possible explanation in *Billboard* magazine: "Since Chinese musicians don't normally have enormous amounts of amplification, the notion that two singers would have an entourage of 85 people must be a little disconcerting, to say the least."

The entourage became even more formidable as time went on. It swelled to over a hundred people in all. This included the whole band, George and Andrew's families, a crew, and over twenty-five cinematographers, plus various journalists. Besides the people, Wham! brought along a measly forty tons of equipment.

The band itself was at the end of its rope physically, only because of the grueling multi-country tour that they were wrapping up with the China dates. The next thing on their schedules was a well-deserved rest. Unfortunately, one of the band members didn't make it into China proper.

Hong Kong was the first stop. Hong Kong is like an island in the middle of China. This bustling city is still owned by the British, and it's totally Westernized. So Wham! had a chance to warm up a bit in a more familiar environment. They felt an intense amount of pressure to get everything letter-perfect; the last thing they needed was bad rumors traveling the short distance to Peking! Poor George was so keyed-up that he expelled a few photographers from his dressing room. It's easy to get nervous before a performance, and the last thing anyone would want is to have someone recording it for posterity.

This incident caused minor alarm, mostly in the press, and the rumors started flying. Speculation was that George was about to fall to pieces because of all the work and responsibility. George himself had other ideas. "Reports that I was crying are a lie," he told *The Sun*. "I'm fine, I'm very happy. Do I look like I'm cracking up?"

Unfortunately, keyboard player Mark Fisher wasn't as

hearty. The overworked musician collapsed after the Hong Kong gigs and never made it behind the bamboo curtain.

Meanwhile, in Peking, people were getting very excited about their British visitors. Like many countries, including the United States, China receives the BBC World Service, which originates in Britain. Through the World Service, a few lucky folks had gotten their first taste of Wham! and they were anxious for more. Other citizens were hearing the word through gossip and the newspapers.

With all this interest, somebody should have made quite a profit, but that somebody definitely wasn't going to be Wham!. "The boys consider it a great honor to be picked as the first Western pop group ever invited to play China. This is a cultural exchange, and making money is not the aim," a representative stated firmly (*The Sun*, March 11).

Good thing it wasn't—for Wham! lost anywhere between $1 million and $1.5 million on the Chinese expedition. One very big cost was the film shot; the entire production cost over $750,000, because it was done so professionally. It was also shot on 35mm film, which is used in all really important movies. An entire twenty-four-track sound recorder was also needed so nary a note would be missed. Luckily for Wham! fans, all those who missed the big event in China will get a chance to see it in the future, in the movies or on video! We'll also get the pleasure of some private moments with Andrew and George as they explore the exotic East.

An additional big expense was transportation. The party had originally planned to travel by bus and see a little more of China. But the plan was deemed impractical, and a Chinese Airways Jumbo Jet had to be chartered for the occasion.

As we've said, money is not allowed to leave China, so the proceeds from the Wham! shows were donated to various cultural organizations and charities. As a result, each show wound up costing the band $500,000. The proceeds themselves wouldn't have helped much even if the band had pocketed them. The two shows netted about $30,000, which is surprising when you do a head count and come up with 17,000 ticket buyers!

That may sound like a very small sum, but the answer lies in the ticket prices. While tickets sold in Hong Kong for about $20, tickets in Peking and Canton sold for somewhere between $1.60 and $1.75! In America, that would be sheer heaven, but in China it takes three days to earn that much.

As a bonus, every ticket buyer received a *Make It Big* cassette. Before they got in line, Chinese fans had to have a note from their work units excusing them from their duties. They also needed a work unit I.D. card, and tickets were issued in blocks of ten to prevent a mob scene.

With Black Market tickets reportedly worth over $50 (figure out how much that is in Chinese terms if you want a big shock), people were eager to get their own from the box office. Over a thousand Chinese people waited on line all through the night to bag the golden tickets. Not long before, Western pop music had been considered "spiritual pollution"; now it was uplifting people's spirits all over Peking!

The Sun, a daily newspaper from Great Britain, interviewed some of the people waiting on line to find out what they thought of all the fuss. One man explained that he was looking for "a better understanding of Western culture."

Tank De'ge, a 29-year-old man who's employed as a factory worker, didn't exactly seem clear about what was going on. "I like Michael Jackson and John Denver," he stated proudly. "Have you heard of Simon and Garfunkel?"

Others waiting in the line were more informed. A 24-year-old student named Ma Zhiliang told *The Sun*: "I have been waiting since 3P.M. yesterday; I have never heard their music. I am sure it will be good." An 18-year-old boy in line commented, "I have not heard their music but the papers say it is good." What a pleasant surprise these people had in store for them!

The Peking show sold out in the speediest possible fashion. When the office finally opened, people cheered. Those in the back of the long line applauded those who got their tickets first. Most of the purchasers were men between the age of 20 and 30 . . . not exactly your typical Wham! audience.

In one part of town, the masses lined up for the pleasure of seeing Wham! onstage. In another part of town, batches of people were seeing Wham! for free, although they weren't performing. The boys were doing a little simple sightseeing, accompanied by their families and the entire entourage! Andrew really stood out in his bright tartan jacket and jazzy gold and black slippers.

One of their stops was the legendary Great Wall of China. It's one of those things that most people find impossible to imagine, because it's over three thousand miles long and more than two thousand years old! Here George and Andrew posed with each other, their families, and their fans. "It's unbelievable that someone should build a wall that's longer than the distance from London to New York," Andy exclaimed in the *Daily Mirror*. George was more awestruck; "Incredible, unthinkable!!" was all he managed to get out.

George had a real spring in his step as he climbed up the wall to have a look around, a little too much spring for Lindsay Anderson, the Wham! documentary director who was trying to follow him. Lindsey slipped and sprained his leg. When George finally came down, *The Sun* newspaper presented him with a medal stating "I Climbed The Great Wall." It's doubtful that George will need anything to remind him of that spectacular visit.

LOVED BY
MILLIONS AND
MORE!

*T*here was a little something missing in Wham!'s Peking show, namely at least half the usual amount of decibels! For China, Wham! were willing to turn down their volume. Loud or soft, Wham! can always get their good-time message across.

Thousands attended the Peking show, but they weren't the kind of Wham! audience you'd find in California or London. The gangs of overheated young women and dancing throngs had been left back at home with the fish and chips. This audience was made up of older officials and army people! An announcer told the assembled crowd to "remain seated and watch with patience."

George's appearance was nothing out of the ordinary.

This guy just can't help looking gorgeous, and this performance was no exception! For the special event, George wore lots of white, and he really looked like an angel. The Chinese were a little disturbed that he wasn't wearing a shirt under his dapper jacket ... perhaps they thought he'd forgotten to put one on. Andrew sported his trademark plaid, and both of the Wham! stars were pictured wearing very Panama-ish hats.

The Chinese were not exactly the wildest audience on earth, but they made the boys feel appreciated. After every song there was very polite applause and some whistles and cheers. Once George tried to get them a bit more into things by clapping along with a song, but the inscrutable ones merely kept up their applause. It was hard for Wham! to communicate anything to their audience, because they didn't have a translator.

The senior officials and other V.I.P. types did have the benefit of translation. They sat in their boxes drinking tea while they watched the proceedings.

This trip was based on goodwill and an exchange of customs, so George and Andrew tried to refrain from expressing their opinion of the Chinese government. But George did make one comment during the concert that was interpreted as being slightly political. He introduced "Freedom" with "We hope that one day it will be Number 1 in China too, with your help."

There were a few disturbances during the concert. Western students who were in the country to study Chinese did what any of us would do when faced with the mighty beat of Wham!—they started dancing. This must have

looked very strange to people who had only seen ballet
and orchestra performances, where no one moves but the
people on stage. Strange or not, several younger Chinese
started to join in.

That's when the trouble started. The police were
alarmed by the odd display and tried to force everyone
back to their seats. British journalist Elain Buckley explained in *The Sun*: "The Brits were having a really wild
time until the police stepped in. China had never seen
anything like it and the officers didn't seem to know how
to cope. They moved off, though, when a cameraman
filmed the clashes. They didn't want to be seen as tough
guys knocking Westerners about."

Eventually everything calmed down, but one unfortunate Chinese fan was arrested. After the show, George
commented on the general atmosphere in *Billboard*: "There
is a huge cultural difference which there's no way to cross
in an hour and a half. It was frustrating to have dignitaries
sitting in front, and I think the younger Chinese were
intimidated by the police."

One V.I.P. in the crowd made no secret of his admi-
ration. British ambassador Sir Richard Evans did a little
moving and shaking in his special box seat. It was plain
that he enjoyed every minute of the extravaganza.

In a different part of the theater, a girl was having her
picture taken for *People* magazine. She proudly displays
a Wham! souvenir scarf...upside down!

After the show, the boys attended a banquet in their
honor. Andrew took the opportunity to say a few words
about the tour and what he felt it was achieving. "This

concert may be a small step for the youth of China; it is a giant step for the youth of the world in bringing our cultures closer together."

CANTON, HERE
WE COME

*T*he next date was to be in Canton, and this concert would end the long tour. The band must have been mighty relieved that the months of wear and tear were about to come to an end. Everyone was in a great mood as the plane left Peking for Canton.

Two people were missing the party. Andrew and George had remained in Peking to do a prerecorded interview for their American fans. It turned out to be a lucky break for the boys, for they didn't have to witness a bizarre incident involving one of their musicians.

It all began with 30-year-old Raoul DeOliviera, a Portuguese trumpeter who had played with the band for at least three years. He was seriously overwrought before the plane took off. Apparently Raoul was hallucinating; he was convinced that he was going to die.

Ten minutes after the plane had left Peking, Raoul completely lost control. He reportedly took a pen knife and began stabbing himself in the abdomen. Then he careened down the aisle and into the cockpit. The startled pilot lost control of the plane, causing it to drop a thousand feet.

Luckily, Chinese planes always carry security guards, and they were able to subdue Raoul. The plane returned to Peking, where the musician received both mental and physical attention. The Wham! tour had to proceed without him, but they were secure in the fact that he was getting the help that he needed.

Naturally George and Andrew were very disturbed about the tragedy. They were especially sorry that their families had been exposed to such a startling experience. But these guys are pros all the way; they put aside their feelings and got on with the show.

Things went much more smoothly once the excitement blew over. The hall was smaller and the people more responsive. The horn section managed to get along without Raoul. As the dynamic show came to a close, George told the cheering crowd: "Thank you, China. This is the best show of the whole tour." It's a wonder the audience let them off after only two encores!

Xiao Hua, the Chinese Vice Minister of Culture, had some words of very high praise for Wham!. He exclaimed that the tour was "the best step forward in Anglo-Chinese relations since the signing of the Hong Kong Treaty."

There was one more task to be completed after the

performances. There was a film to be edited, a film that would show the entire Wham! China saga from successful beginning to supersonic finale. George and Andrew would be flying to L.A. to oversee its progress.

Shooting an amazing event like Wham!'s visit to China is no easy chore. A once-in-a-lifetime happening like this deserved an outstanding crew of professionals.

The documentary will be sixty to seventy-five minutes long, and it was produced by Martin Lewis, who has worked on various video projects, including Julian Lennon's "Much Too Late For Goodbyes." The director, Lindsay Anderson, is responsible for the fine film *O Lucky Man*.

One of Wham!'s comanagers, Jaz Summers, asked Martin to produce the film. Martin was very excited by the whole project. He knew that it couldn't be like any other music documentary. It had to have more than just the usual concert footage and behind-the-scenes shots. He wanted to share the magic of this special event with everyone who wanted to see it, and to create a film that would last for a very long time.

The crew shot sequences featuring the two concerts. They tried to capture some of the more subtle aspects of the affair. The movie will try to catch two views: how the Wham! entourage saw the Chinese and how the Chinese saw Wham!.

Martin Lewis was absolutely enthralled with this weird mixture of cultures. He needed a director who could make the vision really live and breathe, so he went straight to the top of the list and contacted Lindsay, whom he numbers among his favorite directors. Wham! fans who were left at home can look forward to a healthy dose of Wham!'s wonder-cure sound.

POP GO THE
WHAM!ETTES

*T*hey fly to beautiful places in high style, hobnob with the stars, and delight countless people. They wear great clothes, smile great smiles, and execute great dance routines. Night after night they get up onstage with two of the handsomest, most talented, most fabulous guys in the world . . . and they get paid for it! Sounds impossible and exciting, but it's part of the everyday lives of Wham! go-go girls Shirley and Pepsi.

What a life! What a job! What luck! Well, not luck really. Shirley is an old-timer in the Wham! camp; she's one of the people they count among their true friends. She's known Andrew and George since their school days. Her perspective on them is very different from the rest of the world's. When Shirley looks at Andrew she sees a guy with whom she's shared an awful lot of experiences, and some of those experiences have nothing to do with the glam and glitz that surround the duo today. When she looks at George she can see two people. One is a stunning superstar. The other is a scared, overweight little boy with a violin case tucked under his arm.

As long as the boys have people like Shirley around them, they'll never lose track of their roots. So Shirley is more than just a dancer; she's an important anchor aboard the S.S. *Wham!*.

Shirley Pauline Holliman was born on April 18, 1962, in Watford, England. The pretty blonde shares an early interest in music with her coworkers, but she wasn't as interested in Elton John. The first record she bought was an obscure semi-hit called "Dance by the Light of the Moon."

Unlike George and Andrew, Shirley was attracted by the punk movement. She even saw a performance by the Sex Pistols at the famed 100 Club way back in 1976 or '77.

The Sex Pistols were the legendary forerunners of the British punk scene. One of their claims to fame was a single that was banned by BBC Radio. The single was "God Save the Queen," and it rocketed all the way up into the Top 5 of the British charts, setting off a whole explosion of media attention. It's hard to visualize soft and feminine Shirley as a punk, but for a while that's just what she was.

In contrast to her nightclubbing, dressed-up image,

Shirley is an active, outdoorsy kind of girl. She's always loved horses. Though she's held down a few part-time jobs, like waitressing and working for her father (he has his own building business), Shirley's longest-lasting "job" was training to be a riding teacher. Four years of work went into this pursuit. Shirley's sure that if she wasn't a Wham!ette, riding would keep her perfectly content. Many of her friends are four-leg fans too, so she rides with them when her busy schedule permits.

Shirley didn't really get acquainted with Andrew until she was 18. Somehow their paths hadn't really crossed at Bushey Meads. They met in a pub and Shirley recalls finding Andrew very attractive. The two began dating and kept it up for two years despite all sorts of personal friction. George and Andrew were Executives then. Shirley drove them around, because she was the one with access to a car. One of the boys found a way to thank her for those early duties. After Wham!'s initial success, Shirley got an extra-special Christmas gift—a Ford Capri! Coy Shirley refuses to divulge who the generous party is.

This girl on the go is a spitfire, and not prone to sitting around pursuing the scholarly things in life! Shirley is much more into shopping than reading. In the past she's commented that she doesn't want to get so famous that she can't go into her favorite shops . . . maybe it's too late already!

You can see why George and Andrew enjoy the companionship of this high-spirited girl. She'll always have a very special place in their hearts. When the boys first came to America, they were a little concerned about getting up on stage with their two lovely ladies. They were afraid that American girls wouldn't react to Shirley and Pepsi as well as European girls had.

George and Andrew were pleased to find that they were wrong. Wham! audiences did not sprout claws and bulging green eyes at the sight of Wham!'s female cohorts. This proves once and for all that Wham! fans are much more mature than some people think they are.

Realistically, it's hard to imagine how anyone could resent these two bubbly Wham!ettes. A slight shade of envy just doesn't fit into the overall picture of what constitutes a Wham! fan. The feeling of vibrant camaraderie that you get from the foursome onstage and in videos is a real blast. Besides, both girls are attractive in a very inoffensive way. They're not ten tons of perfection and plastic surgery—just nice, normal girls.

Former Wham!ette Dee C. Lee had some interesting comments to make on health and beauty in one of England's most popular girl mags, *Just Seventeen*. Everyone has their little physical problems, but there comes a time when you begin to erase your personality by "correcting" too much. She says that plastic surgery is a terrible idea, because looking completely perfect is very tedious and un-special. "I've been accused of having a lopsided grin," she exclaimed (in *Just Seventeen*). "So what?" There are things you can correct without playing Frankenstein with your own body. These things usually involve other aspects besides the body beautiful. Dee is interested in having her teeth fixed up, for instance. "The bottom row are very crooked, but it's my own fault," she confessed (in *Just*

Seventeen). "When I was at school I had a letter to say I should wear a brace. But I threw it away and never told my mum."

Dee C. had an amicable parting from George and Andrew a couple of years ago, and she now enjoys working on her own solo projects while singing with the Style Council. Before Dee made a living with her music, she made a little money on the side as a model. The kind of modeling Dee did had nothing to do with those full-page pics you see in *Vogue*. Her forte was foot modeling! Her hands and face sometimes appeared in piece work, but her feet were most often used. "Actually, my feet were quite famous in German, Swedish and African magazines," she proudly told *Just Seventeen*.

Let us not forget the fantastic Pepsi, the girl who had to step into Dee's shoes. This girl has faced up to quite a few difficulties on the way to being established as more than just a replacement.

Pepsi joined the group on rather short notice. She didn't have a chance to slide into the glamorous life; she had to dive right in! The group was scheduled to appear a couple of days after she signed on. Pepsi debuted at Capitol Radio's junior "Best Disco in Town," a fun-for-all-ages event staged on a Sunday afternoon at the Lyceum Theatre in London. People came from all over to cheer along with their fave groups, and two thousand lucky folks actually gained entrance to the show that lived up to its name.

Disc jockeys Mike Brown, Kelly Temple, and Wham! supporting jock Gary Crowley tried their darnedest to get the crowd dancing, but "crowd" is putting it lightly. The club was stuffed to the brim. No one could really move, and there were several unfortunate accidents because of this.

Many artists made personal appearances, including Limahl's old band Kajagoogoo. In England and other parts of Europe, a personal appearance usually means that the band comes onstage and mimes to their latest hit. This way, they can get around quickly and see as many of their fans as possible. Wham! decided that the event was the perfect place for Pepsi to get acquainted with the Wham! brigade and vice versa.

Pepsi made a great impression. She and new co-Wham!ette Shirley were healthy and shiny, and they danced together like they'd been at it for ages! The girls looked lovely in their matching white sportswear and white high heels. Everyone agreed that Pepsi was Wham!worthy.

There was only one problem, and luckily it faded away as time bopped on. Pepsi's entrance was so sudden that some of the public were not aware that she'd taken over from Dee. Most fans had only seen the dancers from a distance, when they could bear to tear their eyes away from George and Andrew. People were actually coming up to Pepsi and calling her Dee! In any case, Pepsi is too firmly connected with the boys these days to be confused with anyone else.

What has confused some Wham! fans, however, is what exactly Shirley and Pepsi's position in the group is. Are they part of it? Do they make any decisions? Or are they just hired dancer/singers?

Hired dancer/singers comes the closest to describing their roles. As we've seen, their place is more important than it sounds, but they are more part of the machinery than anything else.

Of course, having two pretty girls on the road can lead to trouble. People can suspect the oddest things ... and they have. Some of the English newspapers find Wham!'s internal workings fascinating, and there's always plenty of gossip flying around.

Shirley is particularly interesting to the English dailies, because she dates very handsome Martin Kemp, who is in the group Spandau Ballet. Once, Shirley even "spilled the beans" in Britain's paper *The Sun*. *The Sun* is famous for its striking headlines and attention-grabbing features. You might think that Andrew and George would be offended by this, but Andrew proved he wasn't when he said, after the article appeared: "She didn't say anything that offended me or wasn't true, I went out with her for two years and I know the difference between her talking and *The Sun* talking."

Shirley has fun with all the media interest. As long as it doesn't hurt anyone, it's okay. She even dropped a line once about her relationship with George. She said he's never been attracted to her, because he favored more buxom women! But occasionally, the gossip is not so harmless ... and that's when a problem can start.

For instance, *The Standard* once reported on a feud that was supposedly brewing between Andrew and Shirley's beau, Martin. The speculation centered around a Wham! gig in Brighton. Shirley was conspicuously absent, and quite a lot of rumors made the rounds. The Wham! publicists explained that it was a very simple matter. Shirley and Andrew had been involved in some spirited hi-jinks before the show and the blond "dancing machine" had hurt herself.

A few nights later the tour closed and the band had a celebratory fiesta. The party was at a high-class club in one of London's subsections, an area called Mayfair (Mayfair is like Boardwalk on the English Monopoly board, very posh indeed!). Shirley and Andrew lowered the tone a bit by indulging in a free-for-all food fight. There goes the neighborhood, but what a way to go!

The next day, Shirley flew off to Australia to see Martin. Spandau Ballet was touring down and receiving ecstatic responses. Of course, Martin wanted her to share the good times with him. By now the news of Shirley and Andrew's "horseplay" had spread. This combined with her no-show at the Brighton gig created a situation where people could come to all sorts of conclusions. One of them seemed to be that Andrew had actually injured his longtime pal. Another concerned Martin's feelings toward Andrew. A source told *The Standard*, "Martin went completely berserk when Shirley told him what happened. You could say that he's very much looking forward to meeting Andrew face-to-face again."

Spandau Ballet's manager Steve Dagger hastened to set the record straight. "I saw Shirley a few days after she arrived in Australia, but I didn't notice any bruising." He explained that Shirley had missed the Brighton show because of a minor spat with the band.

Everyone soon forgot about the series of incidents, and nothing came of it. It's just part of the overall picture of stardom, and it's something that famous people usually have to face.

Shirley did have a real-life accident involving Andrew once, but it was onstage in front of thousands of people. The only thing you could accuse Mr. Ridgeley of in this case was overenthusiastic carelessness in the first degree! You see, Andrew gave a rather vigorous hip flip one night during "Wake Me Up Before You Go-Go" and connected with Shirley. She lost her balance and was flung off into the distance! The poor girl actually ended up with a minor concussion.

Being a Wham!ette can be hazardous to your health! Shirley and Pepsi are more than willing to take the risk, and we don't blame 'em.

After all, who wouldn't dive at the chance to get up and play "let's pretend" with the best of company? One thing's for sure, we all enjoy and appreciate the extra spark Shirley and Pepsi add to Wham!'s stage shows and videos. Their numerous costume changes and rousing rah-rah kind of dancing can bring even the most sluggish watchers to their feet.

AN ABOUT-FACE
FOR ANDREW

When it came to launching pal David Austin's career in pop music, Andrew Ridgeley didn't use his head; he used his nose!

The first reports that appeared in the English dailies were rather frightening. *The Sun*'s front page shouted out the bad news: "Wham! Star Scarred in Brawl at Pop Party."

According to *The Sun*, Andrew was scarred for life. Supposedly, Andrew and David Austin had been in a "fight" over a girl. Their playful pushing and shoving had escalated into a real problem when a champagne bucket went awry and flew in Andrew's face! David told *The Sun*, "I feel terrible about this. . . . We are best mates. . . . He started flirting with my girlfriend, so I poured champagne down his shirt. Andy threw his drink all over me, so I started swinging the ice bucket about. It just slipped out of my hand and hit him in the face."

From his sickbed, Andrew found the strength to tell the paper, "It was just a prank which got out of hand. I forgive Dave and we're still the best of friends."

Actually, the "prank" was more of a lark. When a picture ran in the papers of David and Andrew (with bandaged schnoz) the words under it revealed that Andrew had in reality gone for a nose job. The supposed fight was all a publicity stunt for David, whose first single, "Turn to Gold," was out. Not surprisingly, the single was produced by one George Michael.

As Andrew explained later, the plastic surgery was not a vain indulgence. Since he'd busted his nose as a child, he'd had problems breathing. Poor Andrew was forced into hiding for a bit when Wham! was recording their *Make It Big* LP. Everyone wanted a picture of the most famous nose in recent history!

SPOTLIGHT ON GEORGE MICHAEL

*S*inger/songwriter George Michael has lived through some extraordinary events. He's wowed royalty, thrilled millions, and walked atop the Great Wall of China. These episodes have been shared with Mr. Andrew Ridgeley, and he couldn't have done them without good old Andy by his side. But there are things that George has done on his own, and some of these successes have been very special moments for our hero.

The Apollo Theater is a majestic old building located in the Harlem section of New York City. The Apollo has hosted and launched some of the greatest talents in history. Aretha Franklin, Stevie Wonder, the Jacksons and countless other soul stars have sung and played under its roof. In 1985, dozens of these stars returned to the Apollo as a tribute, and George Michael was with them. Singing with childhood inspiration Smokey Robinson (of the Miracles) was certainly one of George's most rewarding achievements.

Earlier that year, George received another honor. He and Andrew attended a British Music Industry Awards ceremony at London's ritzy Grosvenor House Hotel. The bash was sponsored by the Performing Rights society, and its awards are a real barometer of success.

Andrew and George picked up one award for "Careless Whisper" and were about to settle in and watch the proceedings when Elton John himself announced that another award waited for George! "Very rarely do you meet a major songwriter . . . but this one's in the league of Paul McCartney," Elton proclaimed as he handed George the Ivor Novello award for composition.

George has never been one to hide his emotions, and his joy spilled over as he made a short speech. It made no difference that he cried in front of the show-biz elite! Choked with tears, the handsome hunk spluttered, "As a young songwriter, this award is the most . . . the most important thing I have ever received."

Then he gave Andrew a hug and went off to calm down. Later he commented, "Elton John had just made a tremendous speech that affected me deeply." And who could blame him? George was credited as "the greatest songwriter of his generation" by the man who got him interested in music in the first place.

There are all sorts of different honors in the music industry. Some of them put statuettes on the mantelpiece and money in the bank. Whatever honors George collects in the future, he'll never need anything to remind him of these two nights and the wonderful feelings they gave him.

VISUAL IMPACT WITH A CAPITAL "W"!

*G*eorge and Andrew know how to look great on film. Posing or strutting, smiling or sad, they're walking on sunshine and sharing their dreams with us all. Recently Wham! released their first on-screen compilation. "Wham! The Video" contains such gems as "Wham! Rap," "Bad Boys," "Wake Me Up Before You Go-Go," and "Last Christmas." Now we can watch our favorite Wham! videos over and over.

The compilation is interesting because it goes back to the first video Wham! ever made: "Wham! Rap." Back then, Wham! were bad boys extraordinaire. They had a lion's share of leather, sweat, and motorcycle macho! George accents his sneery vocal with an even sneerier

face as the boys bop through their adventure. George and
Andrew get their message across through bouncy dances;
you don't have to have a job to have fun, and if you can
have fun, then you *are* somebody!

"Young Guns" also takes place in a simple disco setting. Among the whirling lights and rock-steady funk beat,
two friends meet on the dance floor. George is the swinger:
young, free, and single. His friend Andrew used to be as
carefree, but recently he has found another playmate.
He's thrown over his best pal for a girl (portrayed by
Shirley).

In a half-humorous, half-serious rap, George pleads
with Andrew to look before he leaps. He remembers their
good times together. In George's opinion, Andrew isn't
ready for the responsibility of marriage.

Andrew doesn't want to listen, but when Shirley gives
him a royal tongue-lashing moments later, he realizes that
his friend is right. In the end, the boys stick together. It's
a happy ending for everyone but Shirley.

As we see in the next video, bad boys always stick
together. This video was more spoof than serious. "The
'Bad Boys' video was so tongue-in-cheek," laughed
George. And so it was! This little vignette seemed to
praise thumbing your nose at everyone and everything.

The tale is told of bad little boys growing into bad
manhood. As they trade in slingshots for blondes and
fancy cars, they systematically run over every obstacle
in their path, including parents! Didn't George and Andrew's folks find it all a bit upsetting? No, because they
must have known that their sons were just having a laugh.

". . . My parents are intelligent enough to see that," George explained.

The atmosphere at the "Club Tropicana" is a whole nother matter! This video bridged the tremendous gap between Wham!'s tough-guy image and the slick boys they became. For this happy, exotic song a happy, exotic setting was needed. So Andrew and George and Dee and Shirley were all off to film in Ibiza. As you may know, the song itself is about the ultimate nightclub, the best place in the world to be. It's finely illustrated, with a flirtation between the two girls and two boys and a lot of sun, fun, and sand. The video has many striking shots, including one of George and Andrew playing some very wet trumpets. In the surprise ending, George gets a chance to don the pilot's gear he once longed for.

Of course, the first Wham! video you may have seen is the peppy "Wake Me Up Before You Go-Go." Wasn't it every bit as fun as the song itself? Extras for this were found outside the casting offices. Wham! put an ad in a couple of the English papers on the day of the shoot. They invited their fans to show up at a Brixton theater wearing white and carrying something fluorescent.

Wham! were glad they took a chance on their fans, although truthfully it wasn't much of a worry for them. The theater was chock full of enthusiasts, so there was a very good feeling in the air. You can see it on film for yourself. George and Andrew knew that their fans are well behaved and well groomed, and they were right!

"Wake Me Up Before You Go-Go" showed another facet of Wham! on film. Not only had they abandoned their bad-boy image; they had temporarily abandoned lavish sets and play-acting. Simple lighting tricks and an enthusiastic performance were enough to send these guys all the way to number one!

The steamy "Careless Whisper" went back to the method of following the storyline, with fantastic results! The Miami-set saga is enough to take any girl's breath away, and it did. One of the models involved in the dramatic "love triangle" actually fainted during the shoot!

While George was making hearts flutter, Andrew enjoyed a vacation with pal David Austin. Other friends present were Yioda and Melanie and manager Simon Napier-Bell. Andrew and David got to see the sights and hang out on the beach, and George got the most expensive haircut ever. . . .

Videos have budgets, and George's budget for "Careless Whisper" was thirty thousand pounds, give or take a few. George's hair had grown quite long, and the busy boy simply didn't find time to get it cut. In England, he managed to soothe his savage 'do with a blow dryer, but in Miami it wouldn't listen to reason or hot air. The humidity made it uncontrollable, and George couldn't stand it. What's a boy to do?

"I told the producer to start again," George told *No. 1* magazine, "because you want to look nice in your own video, don't you? Fortunately, my sister was with me and she cut my hair on the spot. That haircut cost me 17,000 pounds. . . . I've got the most expensive haircut in the history of pop!" That was because previously shot scenes of George with longer hair didn't match his new look, and needed to be redone.

The opulent hotel where the boys resided during their visit to Miami is a story in itself. The Mutiny Hotel specializes in thematic decor. Every room has a name. Andrew swam around in the Wide Water Room, but George wasn't over the moon about his Lunar Dreams boudoir. "It was more like staying in a disco than a bedroom. There were neon tubes and disco lights all round the bed, a picture of Saturn that lit up one of the walls, and mirrors on the ceiling so that if you were doing anything naughty you could watch!"

Despite these amusing diversions and difficulties, George still managed to make a great video. It tells the classic story of what happens when girl meets boy, boy meets girl ... and boy meets girl. If you are counting that makes one extra girl, and girl number one doesn't take George's indiscretion lying down! It's quite a turnaround from the "Young Guns" days when George was encouraging Andy to dump his steady in favor of the wild life.

When "Last Christmas" wasn't released in America, Wham! fans missed out on a very special video. It is available on the Wham! video compilation, but it would have been really nice to see it on TV. A surprise dose of Wham! is always welcome, and the lovely settings added something Wham!-derful to the holiday season.

For "Last Christmas" the boys took their friends, including the Wham!ettes and George's companion Pat Fernandez, to a snowy ski resort. The gang wine and dine and have snowball fights, but their cheerfulness is only a backdrop to a sad story. George finds that the girl he loves has deserted him for Andrew. Andrew is even wearing a brooch that George had given her.

Beside their own Christmas video, Wham! can also be seen on BandAid's "Do They Know It's Christmas?" video. This cooperative effort shows the boys sharing another kind of Christmas spirit, the spirit of giving.

On "Everything She Wants" the sound is BIG. So the boys complied by intermixing filmed footage with one of their super BIG concerts! The lighting on this exciting video is beautiful, very soft and moody. George and Andrew appear for lots of sexy close-ups, and there's only one thing missing . . . color! Nobody's complaining, however. . . .

The scenes that accompany "Freedom" are a preview of the Wham! in China documentary. Scenes of Oriental cultural highpoints, ominous policemen, twirling dancers, and other notable aspects of the China dates (especially George and Andrew!) make for a spectacular video that's more than just a promotional film. The "Freedom" video is a little bit of history.

On the beach, in the clubs, or in stark black and white, Wham! is a treat. Their high-quality video performances will always be something to look forward to.

EPILOGUE

Will George and Andrew ever get sick of seeing their names linked with the number one? Not very likely! Wham! fought hard to get to the top, and they're settled in for a long time. It's hard to imagine the contender who could manage to knock these two off their thrones.

Wham! belong to the world, because they are far too talented to belong to any small group of people. Wham! also belong to you and you alone, because big talent is a mixture of different ingredients. There's something for everyone in Wham!'s music.

No matter how famous they get, and no matter how many records they sell, George and Andrew have always realized that the masses of bodies they see in stadiums are made up of individuals. The magic of Wham! means different things to different people, but one feeling is shared by all when it comes to George and Andrew ... Wham! is forever.

WHAM!ARAMA

- Andrew once had a wheel of his Ford Capri spray-painted gold. The car has since been retired for service above and beyond.
- Wham!'s video for "Bad Boys" is inspired by the movie of *West Side Story*.
- The "Wham! Rap!" demo only cost the boys twenty pounds to make.
- George hates being stared at.
- In spite of his appearance, Andrew isn't fond of sun-bathing. He gets brown by playing on the beach, not lying on it. Both he and George tan easily.
- Until 1985, both George and Andrew lived at home. In the summer of '85, George bought an apartment but

couldn't go shopping to get it fixed up. Every time he entered a store there was a mob scene.

- Jenny Ridgeley keeps scrapbooks of Wham!'s clippings.
- Lesley Michael used to run the group's fan club.
- George played bass on the "Wham! Rap" demo; Andrew programmed the drum machine.
- Even after Wham! had chalked up a few hits, George's dad was convinced that it was all a passing thing. He's happy the boys proved him wrong.
- "If You Were There" is an old Isley Brothers song.
- George is planning his next solo single; it's a song he wrote long ago, titled "Stephen."
- One reason for the delays when "Bad Boys" was being recorded was illness. Poor George had a nasty encounter with the flu.
- After that historic "Top of the Pops" appearance, "Young Guns" really went for it! Sixty thousand copies were sold on the peak day.
- David Austin used to appear on TV with Wham!
- Before they were worldwide stars, Wham! bad-guy image inspired a small group of clones. They called themselves "Wham!boys."
- Wham! was almost managed by the same people who handle the Jacksons.
- Paul Ridgeley did some drumming on *Fantastic*.
- Albert Mario has been involved in computer work. He's also worked for Canon, the camera company.
- "Wake Me Up Before You Go-Go" has been number one in America, England, Holland, Belgium, Australia, Denmark, Norway, Austria, and Ireland, to name but a few!

- Andrew once tried to learn to play the piano when he was a boy.
- George's answering machine used to have a very confusing message from his dad recorded on it. "Most people put the phone down halfway through the message— which was the general idea."
- Wham! did a personal appearance to help families of Britain's striking miners in the fall of 1984.
- George and Andrew promoted "Last Christmas" by dressing up. George played Santa, and Andy was a reindeer.
- "Do They Know It's Christmas?" sold out on its first day in the stores.
- The "Last Christmas" video was shot in Geneva, Switzerland.
- Wham! gets bombarded with stuffed koala and kangaroo toys when they play in Australia.
- George once did the town with Liza Minnelli after she'd watched the guys rehearse in Hollywood. There was even some talk of George composing songs for her!
- George almost bought the late actress Diana Dors's mansion in England. Diana Dors was Britain's answer to Marilyn Monroe, and she was still very famous when she died.
- Andrew was in Australia for his twenty-first birthday, so he flew a few friends Down Under for a celebration.
- Four songs that were recorded for *Fantastic* got thrown out before the album was finished.
- On the "Club Fantastic" tour, Wham! got their kicks by sticking shuttlecocks (the things you hit in badminton)

down their shorts onstage! Some members of the press were really aggravated by these antics, and made quite a lot of fuss about it. Wham! just laughed.

- George Michael is the first person to ever score consecutive number ones in Britain with both a group and a solo single.
- George once tried working for his dad, but he was dismissed for mixing up the drink orders.
- Most of Wham!'s musical influences are American.
- George hates "Bad Boys" these days, but Andrew still thinks it's a pretty neat dance record.
- Jenny's father was also inclined toward water sports. Andrew's grandfather rowed on a crew team for England.
- "Careless Whisper" was originally produced by soul legend Jerry Wexler, but that version was not used, and George took it back to England to redo. The entire production cost over £200,000!
- Melanie Michael styles hair in a very posh salon in Knightsbridge. She takes care of Andrew-'n'-George's make-up for stage and photos.
- Wham! recorded *Make It Big* in France partially because it took some pressure off them, taxwise.
- George doesn't really like making videos, and he's not as fond of touring as Andrew is.
- George loves kids, and he thinks he'd like to have two boys.
- Andrew's favorite pin-up girl used to be Brooke Shields. "I just love glamorous brunettes," he once confided.
- Wham!'s manager, Simon Napier-Bell, has written a tell-all autobiography called *You Don't Have to Say You*

Love Me. He once tried to get a club disc jockey fired because the guy wouldn't play any Wham! records.

- It cost Wham! a staggering £100,000 to be released from their Innervision contract.
- Wham!'s tour sponsor, Fila, eventually asked the boys to stop wearing their product. Fila clothes are too expensive for a lot of folks to buy, and since the boys had made them popular, people had resorted to shoplifting to imitate the look!
- The video for "Wake Me Up . . ." was produced by John Roseman and directed by Duncan Gibbens. Duncan also directed the videos for the singles from *Fantastic*.
- Wham! performed "Young Guns" on "American Bandstand." It was one of their first American appearances.
- George enjoys drinking his tea with honey.
- In early 1985, George was forced to cancel a sold out Wham! show because he hurt his back. Later he admitted that he didn't know exactly how the injury occurred, but it was either his onstage performance or his backstage Madonna impersonation!
- George admits that bits of "Bad Boys" was inspired by a song called "Tell Me That I'm Dreaming" by Detroit's Was (Not Was).
- George wears a "YOG" ring that his parents gave him.
- George took violin lessons for six years.
- Andrew has been searching for a residence near the Thames River. His grandparents once lived near the Thames.
- Andrew's least-fave Wham! tune is "A Ray of Sunshine."
- Andrew enjoys watching Wham! on TV. (Who doesn't!?)

- Jenny once received a very extravagant present from Andrew: an Alfa Romeo Sprint! Nothing but the best for Mom!

- George wrote a song called "Wham!shake" that was supposed to be their comeback tune, but it was scrapped and replaced with "Wake Me Up..."

- Andrew has played soccer with the equally soccer-crazed Rod Stewart.

- George and Andrew thoroughly grossed out American journalist Suzan Colon (from *Star Hits* magazine) by introducing her to the European tradition of eating chips (french fries) with mayonnaise. Do not attempt this dangerous trick without adult supervision!

- Nothing scares George more than overeager fans who risk life and limb to get near him. He shudders when he recalls how one girl almost had her arm slammed in their limo door.

- At the "Wake Me Up Before You Go-Go" promotional party, CBS gave away black and red yo-yos with tiny doll records pasted on the side.

- Andrew likes Eau Savage and Chanel aftershave.

- Andrew was involved in a car crash in 1984. He gallantly accepted full responsibility (to the tune of £2,000). A friend of the other party told *The Sun*: "He was tickled that it was Andy he was in an accident with, but his car did major work." What a way to meet a star!

- When Simon Napier-Bell invited a Chinese official out for dinner to discuss Wham!, he got more than he bargained for; the guy turned up with 120 other officials! The dinner reportedly cost Napier-Bell £10,000.

- Albert Mario is an amateur photographer, and he's even exhibited some of his pictures.
- The boys were thrilled to take part in the London half of the historical Live Aid concert. George even got to sing with his hero Elton John; he performed "Don't Let the Sun Go Down on Me."
- George sang backing vocals on David Cassidy's comeback single "The Last Kiss."
- George's favorite song on *Make It Big* is "Everything She Wants."
- "Wake Me Up . . ." was nominated for a Grammy award.
- George has confessed that he's partial to blondes, but a girl's looks are not all that important to him.
- George used to get very nervous and start smoking, but it became more of a habit and he must have realized what it might do to his sweet, soulful voice if he kept at it. He hasn't gone near a cigarette in ages.
- Jack's real first name is Kyriacos.
- Japanese fans throw sweets at yummy Wham! to show their appreciation.
- David Austin had a rather embarrassing time one night onstage with the guys. Some joker squirted shaving cream down his pants, and the poor boy fairly oozed onstage!
- George's teeth are in much better shape than Andrew's. They're naturally strong, and he only has a couple of fillings.
- Wham! is the first act since the Beatles to have consecutive number ones in the U.S. and Britain!
- George Michael has appeared onstage with the outrageous band Frankie Goes To Hollywood, in the U.K.

- Once, George wouldn't listen to sister Melanie's advice and he dyed his hair BLACK. "He got a real shock when he saw himself," she commented. "Our dad wouldn't sit at the same table as him."
- Andrew is good friends with English pop star Nick Hayward. Nick used to front a band called Haircut 100, but these days he's solo.
- Andrew adores actress Karen Allen.
- Andrew wants marriage and children, but he won't say when.
- George thinks he'll get married when he's in his late twenties.
- Andrew enjoys British comedian Rowan Atkinson.
- One of George's most memorable childhood presents was a blue and purple bike.

LIFE FILE FOR ANDREW JOHN RIDGELEY

BIRTHDAY: January 26, 1963
HAIR: Brown
EYES: Brown
WEIGHT: 170
HEIGHT: 6 feet, 2 inches
BORN: Surrey (Windlesham, specifically)
SIGN: Aquarius
FAMILY: Parents Albert Mario and Jenny, and brother Paul
PETS: Andrew is fond of cats.
FAVE COLOR: Blue
FAVE CAR: Ferrari
HOBBIES: Football, watching television, and driving fast!
FAVE DRINK: Red wine

SPORTS: Football and motor car racing, natch! Plus badminton, volleyball, and swimming.

FOREIGN LANGUAGES: A bit of French and a smaller bit of German.

TIME BORN: Five-thirty in the A.M.

FIRST ONSTAGE EXPERIENCE: When Andrew was a wee little boy, he appeared in a grade school play or two, including *Joseph and the Amazing Technicolor Dreamcoat*. Later, he went on to play Satan in *The Prodigal Son*. He had to sing two songs and he did quite well, but he couldn't keep the words straight. Andrew is still interested in acting.

READING: Andrew enjoys humorous British author Tom Sharpe.

FIRST ALBUM: "Goodbye Yellow Brick Road," by Elton John.

FIRST SINGLE: Either "Wig Wam Bam," by the Sweet, or "Popcorn"

FIRST SONG PLAYED ON GUITAR: "The Forest," by an English band called the Cure, when Andrew was around 17.

NICKNAME: Ange

LIFE FILE FOR GEORGE MICHAEL

BIRTHDAY: June 25, 1963

HAIR: Two-tone brown with blond streaks

EYES: Lightish brown

WEIGHT: 160

HEIGHT: 6 feet

BORN: In Finchley, North London

SIGN: Gemini

FAMILY: Parents Lesley and Jack, sisters Yioda and Melanie

PETS: George is fond of cats.

FAVE DRINK: White wine

FAVE COLORS: Blue and brown

FAVE CAR: Mercedes and Rolls

SPORTS: Badminton, George likes to exercise onstage!

HOBBIES: Really normal stuff that most people take for granted. With George's busy schedule, it's a treat for him to go out for dinner or a spin on the dance floor.

SOCKS: George buys his socks from the British chain store Marks and Spencer.

JOBS: Movie theater usher, disc jockey, and stockroom boy at British Homes Stores (another chain). Even though he was out of sight, the employers insisted that George wear a tie. He refused and got fired. In 1982, George DJ'ed at the Green Dragon in Croydon, Surrey. The club featured special disco nights that were run by his cousin Andreas Georgiou and some partners. Wham! was signed by then, but George enjoyed himself. "He used to play his own records something chronic," a participant recalled (*The Sun*).

NICKNAME: Yog

DISCOGRAPHY

A Wonderful Wham! Discography, or, What's Shaking at the Club Tropicana

British Singles

Wham! Rap (Enjoy What You Do)/Wham! Rap (Club Mix)
Young Guns (Go For It)/Going For It
Bad Boys/ Bad Boys Instrumental
Club Tropicana/Blue (Armed With Love)
Club Fantastic Megamix: A Ray of Sunshine/Come On!/Love Machine
Wake Me Up Before You Go-Go/Wake Me Up Instrumental
Careless Whisper/Careless Whisper Instrumental
Freedom/Freedom Instrumental
Last Christmas/Everything She Wants

British Albums

Fantastic
Bad Boys
A Ray of Sunshine
Love Machine
Wham! Rap (Enjoy What You Do)
Club Tropicana
Nothing Looks The Same In The Light
Come On!
Young Guns (Go For It)
Make It Big
Wake Me Up Before You Go-Go
Everything She Wants
Heartbeat
Like A Baby
Freedom
If You Were There
Credit Card Baby
Careless Whisper

American Singles

Bad Boys/Bad Boys Instrumental
Wake Me Up Before You Go-Go/Wake Me Up
    Instrumental
Careless Whisper/Careless Whisper Instrumental
Everything She Wants/Like a Baby

American Albums

Fantastic
Bad Boys
A Ray of Sunshine
Love Machine
Wham! Rap (Enjoy What You Do)
Club Tropicana
Nothing Looks The Same In The Light
Come On!
Young Guns (Go For It)
Make It Big
Wake Me Up Before You Go-Go
Everything She Wants
Heartbeat
Like A Baby
Freedom
If You Were There
Credit Card Baby
Careless Whisper

VIDEOGRAPHY

Videos

Wham! Rap
Young Guns (Go For It)
Bad Boys
Club Tropicana
Wake Me Up Before You Go-Go
Careless Whisper
Last Christmas
Everything She Wants
Do They Know It's Christmas?
Freedom

Compilation Videos

Wham! The Video

FAN CLUB INFORMATION

Write to Wham!
c/o Columbia Records
1801 Century Park West
Los Angeles, CA 90067

ABOUT THE AUTHOR

Darlene Fredricks lives with her sister Marci in a former Launderette in New York City. Her hobbies include fencing, rock climbing, listening to Wham!, and trying to teach the cat to meow.

ROCK IS HERE TO STAY...
SO STAY IN TOUCH WITH THE HOTTEST ROCK STARS!

A behind-the-scenes look that is sure to please even the most well-informed fan